Entertaining at Home

To Ernestine Raclin
with best wishes
Enjoy

For Bea and Pat
to their good life together

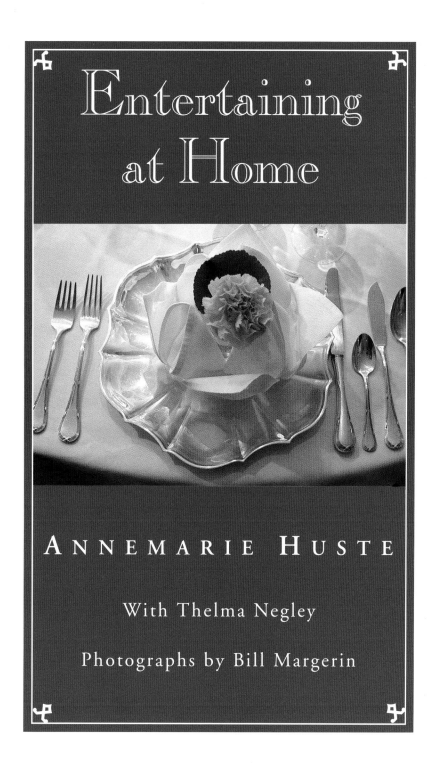

Entertaining at Home

ANNEMARIE HUSTE

With Thelma Negley

Photographs by Bill Margerin

HARRY N. ABRAMS, INC., PUBLISHERS

Project Director: Darlene Geis
Editor: Lory Frankel
Designer: Rhea Braunstein
Food Stylist: Delores Custer

Library of Congress Cataloging-in-Publication Data

Huste, Annmarie.
Entertaining at home / by Annemarie Huste with Thelma Negley.
p.   cm.
ISBN 0-8109-2581-8
1. Entertaining.   2. Cookery.   3. Menus.
I. Negley, Thelma.   II. Title.
TX 731.H87   1990
642'.4—dc20   90-136
CIP

Clothbound edition published by Harry N. Abrams, Inc., under the title
To the Good Life! Entertaining with Annemarie

CONTENTS

The foyer of Annemarie's brownstone is always filled with dramatic flower arrangements

A charming trompe l'oeil *mural of the country beckons toward the coatroom*

INTRODUCTION

E VER since I can remember, I have dreamed of being a cook. At the age of sixteen, after serving a three-year apprenticeship in shoe sales and business administration—what my mother considered a *real* profession—I began an apprenticeship in cooking. In those days in Germany it wasn't yet glamorous to become a professional cook, especially not for a woman, but I always loved it and sensed that there were endless opportunities in the field—although not necessarily in Germany.

So I arrived in America at the age of nineteen, with three dollars in my pocket and less English. After working a year as an *au pair* girl (which means you do everything for the family that sponsors you), I decided I was ready to make a success of myself. I found my first position as chef to a Greek shipping family. I had a great time until I got bored peeling grapes for eight, and I went on to become chef and, later, executive housekeeper to the late Billy Rose.

It was with Billy Rose that my career really began. Making elegant dinner parties for some of the great in show business, I blossomed as a chef. Mr. Rose loved the fact that he employed, as he used to call me, the youngest gourmet chef (I was twenty-one).

After Billy Rose died, I had the good fortune to become chef to Mrs. John F. Kennedy, who had just moved from Washington, D.C., to New York. Talk about success! Here I was, twenty-two years old, and working for a woman with more taste and style in entertaining than anyone I had ever met—or have met since.

I learned a tremendous amount with Mrs. Kennedy the two years I spent there. After that, I wrote my first cookbook and started my own cooking school. I have been food editor for *Saturday Evening Post* and the German edition of *Family Circle*. I traveled around the country teaching my Cookingschool courses, wrote three more cookbooks, opened a food take-out shop, starred in several television cooking shows, became executive chef to *Gourmet* magazine. My early training in shoe sales and business administration stood me in good stead: I knew enough about bad feet to wear sensible shoes during work, and it made running a business much easier.

While working in these and dozens of other food-related endeavors, learning every aspect of food preparation and its business, the one that remained closest to my heart was entertaining, whether for business or for friends. I have always loved—as I do still—nurturing people, making them feel special, so it is only natural that I ended up entertaining professionally. From a town house that contains my living quarters, I run a private dining room that caters primarily to business groups. The fact that it is also my home gives a warmth to the space that makes my clients feel comfortable.

I don't believe there is anyone who enjoys his or her business more than I do mine; in fact, I consider it my bliss. Looking back to when I arrived here twenty-six years ago, I never would have believed just how happy I would become.

Being in this business, I am always approached for advice about entertaining. I decided to sit down and write this book to share with you my joy in and knowledge of giving a party. Once you know a few rules, you will see how easy and how much fun it is.

The foundation of entertaining is good food, well prepared, so the bulk of this book is recipes. One of the reasons my cookbooks have been so popular is that the people who used them found my recipes were not only easy to follow but also that they came out delicious without requiring a lot of equipment or money. Many of my favorite recipes from these earlier cookbooks are included here, for several reasons: they are just as good now as they were then; the books are no longer available; and a whole new generation has grown up since the first one was published twenty-one years ago.

Those of you who have the earlier cookbooks will be happy to learn that some of the old recipes have been updated to take advantage of new equipment as well as foods that weren't then available. I can remember making a salmon mousse by putting the fish through the grinder twice, then forcing the ground salmon through a sieve, then adding the cream drop by drop while beating it over iced water—not too much fun! Now my food processor does all of this in two minutes.

My old friends will also be happy to learn that my basic philosophy about food has remained the same. I still believe that "you only get out of it what you put into it": old vegetables do not grow younger in a pot, and inferior ingredients do not improve on being cooked. I also still believe there is no point in trying things you do not enjoy making; they will never come out terrific. (This is one of the reasons why you will find here few recipes for hors d'oeuvres or breakfasts; I prefer to have someone else do these.)

I would like this book to be more than a collection of recipes: it offers my idea of what I think entertaining should be. If at times I come off as opinionated, I hope you will forgive me and realize it arises from my enthusiasm for the subject as well as my knowledge, gained over the years, of what works best. Having been fortunate enough to learn from the very best and to cook for kings and queens, presidents and chairmen of the board from all around the world, I have gained a wealth of experience, and I am eager to share my joy of entertaining well with you. Because when you are having a good time, so will your guests, and knowing how to do something well gives you a good time.

ENTERTAINING WITH EASE

I find that more people entertain at home today than ever before. I can well understand why, since nothing can match the intimacy of one's own home shared with friends. That does not mean that you have to cook everything yourself; today, many kinds of ready-to-serve foods are available to augment your own.

No matter how you entertain, one of the most important guidelines to remember is to be organized; it makes it all so much easier. Entertaining is 80 percent organization. I am a great believer in lists. Using lists as backup, it is hard to forget anything in the heat of the evening, and having it all laid out on paper will relax and reassure you.

The first thing to do is create a plan. Decide what kind of a party it is going to be. This depends on how much room you have and how many people you want to invite. If you have a table that can seat only eight but you need to invite twelve people, then make it a buffet—or how about a soup party? I did that once, for the publication of my second book. I had different soups on my stove, and everybody loved sampling them. If you have the room but lack supplies, you can always rent such things as tables and china. For myself, I prefer making two small parties rather than one large one.

The next item on the agenda is to put together a menu. The menu should accord with the style of the party. Unless you are adventurous or very knowledgeable, you are best off choosing recipes with which you are most comfortable. Rather than venturing to make dishes you have never made before, stick with the ones that you enjoy making and that people enjoy eating. I also suggest not using more than two dishes that call for last-minute preparation, which tends to create stress. Another aid is to take advantage of the range and quality of prepared foods. These can easily fill in one of the courses, especially dessert or the appetizer. I have always felt that if others can do something as well as I can do it, I'll go ahead and let them, leaving myself free to do the things they can't—such as showing my guests a good time. You may also involve your guests in the preparation of the meal. If your kitchen is large enough, invite your guests in either to watch or participate in the preparation while they nibble on a delicious hors d'oeuvre. People love to do this, and it sets an air of festive informality and coziness.

Above all, it is important to keep your perspective—this is only a meal, not a summit talk on which the peace of the world depends. In other words, relax! If, despite all your planning, something should go wrong, do the best you can to correct it and then forget it.

Annemarie the hostess chats with a guest during dinner

Annemarie the chef prepares the filling of mushrooms, red and yellow peppers, wild rice, and pine nuts for the stuffed squabs

Preparing a bread pudding, one of the desserts

After you have planned the menu, make a shopping list, going over each recipe that you have selected. Make sure that the ingredients you think you already have are indeed at hand. Last-minute trips to the store are no fun. Remember to include garnishes.

Make a list of the pots and pans you need. You do not want to discover at the last minute that one of your pots is too small or that you need the same pot for two different uses simultaneously. Go over your recipes in terms of the number of burners on your stove that you will need as well as oven space, to make sure you can accommodate them all. Next check your dishware, glasses, serving plates, and linen. Make sure they are adequate for your needs and clean. If you do not have to worry about children knocking things over or you do not need the table for breakfast or lunch, set your table the night before—unless you are lucky enough to have staff that can do it two hours before your guests arrive.

A word about my second favorite subject after cooking—flowers. I personally don't enjoy my meal as much if I don't have fresh flowers at my table and in the rest of the house. I think flowers can transform the most simple abode and add to the most elegant space. Whether you order the arrangements from your favorite florist or you arrange them yourself, make sure that you plan this part ahead of time as well, particularly if you want specific flowers.

The wines you serve depend, of course, on your menu, pocketbook, and the occasion you are celebrating. I have a wonderful wine store whose owner makes suggestions on what would be most appropriate; no one can be expert on everything, and wine is, after all, his business. In fact, I rely greatly on all of my suppliers to give me their best. I have bribed them for years by occasionally bringing them my famous fudge brownies. They work so well that I have managed to make my part of New York City my own little town.

With all these things taken care of, it's time to invite your guests—unless you have already done so. If you are giving an important business party, it ought to be somewhat formal. As most people have crowded schedules, your invitations should be early. Family get-togethers, of course, are much less formal; you can just call up to invite your guests. For a gathering of friends, you may go for either casual or elegant or any degree in between, depending on the occasion, your mood, and the group of friends involved. I might add my own solution for obligatory entertaining: I get them all together, rent a restaurant room, and plan a good menu with the chef there. It may simply be easier to set such gatherings in a neutral space.

Finally, try to have some hired help, even if it is only one person for cleaning up. There are many teenagers and other willing people out there looking for ways to earn money, and you will enjoy the evening much more if you are not dreading the cleanup.

In all my planning, my overall rule of thumb is: be truly generous. I buy the best, freshest ingredients I can find, and I serve the best wines I can afford. A little extra spent on flowers or decorations makes a big difference in creating a festive atmosphere. Over the years, I have learned that whatever I give, I get back. Among friends, I reap goodwill. When it comes to business, I have gotten what I wanted (including a million-dollar bank loan!). A beautiful table setting, glowing candles, flowers, lovely garnishes can make even the simplest meal into a warm and memorable occasion.

Stuffing the squabs

Planning and Organizing in Detail

Once you have decided on the kind of party to give, what the menu will be, and how many people you will have, more detailed planning is helpful.

When putting together your menu, think also in terms of what is in season. Although in most cities it is possible to get almost any fresh ingredient any time of the year, I personally prefer to use ingredients that are in season. I look forward to the first local asparagus or the first fresh peaches. My Butternut Squash and Apple Soup, which I start serving in late September, is loved by everyone. Serving such foods in season is special, and an added benefit is their lower cost.

Annemarie trusses the squabs before roasting them

If you should decide to rent tables, chairs, or other items, be sure to reserve them early enough; you don't want to find out at the last minute that the particular items you want are unavailable. Before ordering, go through your entire menu to make sure you remember all the dishes and accessories you'll need. Don't forget the large coffee urn, unless you own one yourself. Remember to ask about the rental store's policies regarding delivery, pickup, and washing up. Try to have the rental items delivered the day before or early on the day of the party. Then have someone available to move furniture if necessary and to help you set up. I suggest when renting china, glasses, and silver not to mix it with your own; it is too aggravating to sort it out later. Another advantage in renting is that ordinarily you only have to rinse, not wash, the dishes. Several days before the party, check to see if your own silver needs polishing or your china, crystal, or other accessories need washing or dusting.

Decide which dishes on your menu can be made ahead of time. Most soups, for instance, come to no harm when made several days earlier or even frozen the week

A golden bread pudding emerges from the oven

before. Sorbets and most mousses can be made up to two days before (gelatin-based mousses or soufflés tend to become rubbery after two days).

The day before the party, make a schedule of all the things that need to be done in the order that they should be done. Take your menu and note the time that each dish will be made, put into the oven, removed, taken out of the refrigerator, and warmed up. Also note what garnishes each dish calls for. Post this list on the refrigerator. I still do this myself, even though I routinely entertain three or four times a week.

On the day of the party, if you could not set your table the night before, then at least try to do it in the afternoon. Prepare all your garnishes, such as chopping parsley and snipping chives. Line up all the pots and pans you will be using, and place serving dishes in a warmer if you have one. Generally, do as much as you possibly can an hour before your guests arrive to give you time to change and take a breather. It will make your evening immeasurably more relaxed and enjoyable.

Help

If you are fortunate enough to have regular help, it will, of course, make entertaining a lot easier. Unfortunately, few people have that luxury these days. That means hiring people for each event.

There are many different sources of help, depending on the area you live in and your budget. You can advertise, go through an agency, or contact high schools and colleges. In some areas, the Youth Employment Service runs "party helper" courses for students. It is a good idea to meet whomever you hire a few days before the party; avoid hiring someone sight unseen. Once you have found help that you like, try to get them for the next party, as it will make it much easier.

Whenever I hire helpers, I always look at their personalities first. I have found that if the person has the right attitude, you can teach him or her anything. On the other hand, an experienced worker with a sour disposition can upset your evening. Next, you should take the time to explain to your help what the occasion is all about—whether it's for business or friends, the mood you want to set. Go over every detail of the event, including the menu, how you would like everything served, and what time to serve things.

Make a list for the help as well. I have put together a typed list, enclosed in plastic, that explains everything that needs to be done before and as the guests arrive. It runs through each course of the menu, specifying when each dish should be served, which garnishes, serving pieces, and utensils to use for each dish, and ends with giving the coats to the guests as they leave. Every time I entertain, each of my butlers goes over it, even those who have been with me for a long time, so as not to forget anything. It also serves as a handy reference, so the staff won't have to interrupt to ask questions.

The most important tip I have in dealing with hired helpers is to treat them with courtesy and respect. Having worked for many years in private households as an employee and been an employer myself for many years, I can assure you it makes a tremendous difference. Make sure to have food for your help; nobody works well while hungry. I have learned that if you take good care of them, they will take good care of you. Giving someone an extra tip for excellent work always helps, particularly if you have regular live-in help. If something should go wrong, handle it quietly and with a sense of humor so you don't make anybody feel uncomfortable.

Guests

The secret of being a successful hostess is to make your guests feel special. Remembering a preferred brand of scotch, a favorite dish, or that someone drinks tea seems like a small detail. However, these are the little particulars that show you care, and they make a wonderful impression. When I worked for Jacqueline Kennedy (now Onassis), I learned this faculty from my employer, who was known for it. If you do a lot of entertaining you might want to keep a small notebook listing such things, as well as the menu you served for which guests.

When planning a party, consider the mix of guests. A little diversity makes for an interesting evening, as long as they all get along. Having too many people will make everyone uncomfortable and lower their enjoyment. I try to keep my cocktail hour to half an hour and never let it get beyond one hour before dinner. You don't want your guests either to get too hungry or to have that one extra drink that will keep them from enjoying the meal. When serving drinks, generosity is not necessarily a virtue. It is better to mix them on the weak than on the strong side. This is particularly important when your guests arrive by car. You may handle this situation humorously or seriously, but be assured that you are doing your guest a favor.

Serving

When you do have someone helping you in the kitchen and sufficient staff for serving, you could have French service, which simply means that the waiters go around the table offering the food from platters. I do not serve this way, since I usually find that by the time everybody has received a portion the food is cold. It also requires staff that knows how to serve this way and that is strong enough to carry heavy platters. In addition, both staff and guests often find French service awkward.

I plate the food in the kitchen, preheating plates when I'm serving hot food. By plating the food, I can arrange the various items beautifully on the plate. (When serving, the meat portion should be at the bottom of the plate, facing the guest.) This type of service is generally faster, assuring that the food will be hot for each person.

Whichever way you decide to serve, make sure you have given your help specific and detailed instructions; do not assume they know exactly what to do.

If you have little or no help, you could serve the food family style, passing platters around the table, or make the dinner a buffet. In either case, try to keep the food as hot as possible. Chafing dishes are very helpful in this regard.

The following chapters on the elements of entertaining—table settings, cutlery, glasses, lighting, and so on—are ideas that I have found work well for me in my private dining room. Since I have the privilege of getting excellent advice from an in-house florist and bartender, I thought that you might enjoy their expertise as well.

The soup is served

The first course, Seafood Sausage (page 24), is placed before a guest

A waiter pours wine to accompany the main course

The main course is served

Presenting the desserts

Annemarie and her chef Walter arrange the roasted squabs on dinner plates

Walter adds the finishing touches to salad with goat cheese

SETTING THE MOOD

❧

The tables are set with fresh flowers, sparkling goblets, and napkins folded into Annemarie's signature lotus

EVER since I can remember I have loved a beautifully set table. It makes eating twice as much fun, and you can create any mood you wish. I remember setting romantic dinner tables just for two, and getting anything I wanted from him afterward. I also remember when I got my first apartment in New York City (while working for Jackie Kennedy), I gave a party for my friends when I did not yet have any furnishings, only wall-to-wall carpeting. I laid out a beautiful tablecloth on the floor, placed on it a silver candelabra that I had rented, created a lovely flower arrangement, and used elegant china, glasses, and silver (also rented; it was cheaper to rent things in those days). A great time was had by all. Now I no longer have to worry about those things; I have plenty of tables, chairs, china, silver, and glasses, and I enjoy setting beautiful tables more than ever.

How you set your table depends on what you like and what you have. If you have two different services for six, you might combine them in alternating patterns. I personally love to use lots of flowers, but you can make a striking centerpiece with colorful fruits or vegetables or your favorite objects. On one occasion, when I put together a special surprise birthday party for one of the leading hostesses in New York, to which guests from all around the world were flown in, I used centerpieces of large geodes, shimmering rose quartz, crystals, and amethysts. In between them I piled rock salt, in which I partly buried votive candles in glass containers, and then I scattered orchids around. We even changed the lighting to highlight the centerpiece. The overall effect was magic, and I loved the fact that I could dazzle such a cosmopolitan group.

A mirrored wall reflects the dining room

A beautiful arrangement of flowers in the dining room helps set the festive mood

People always ask me where all my ideas come from. Some simply come to me; others I get from magazines, books, and people. I have collected table-setting ideas for years in my files. My secret is that I have always been willing to learn from the best.

To cover the table, I have a colored undercloth that goes to the floor and on top of it I place a white cotton or linen cloth. I use cotton or linen for my napkins as well, since they feel much more comfortable on my mouth than does polyester. My napkins are slightly starched, because I fold them in a lotus shape in which I then place a small vase with a single flower. I included the fold in this book since my guests invariably ask me how to do it (see page 10).

Cutlery

The question I am most often asked about table settings with multiple forks and spoons is, "Where should they be placed?" Here is a basic rule to follow: place the one to be used first on the outside, then the others in successive order. If you begin with a salad, the salad fork goes on the outside left-hand side, followed by the fish fork and ending with the dinner fork closest to the plate. On the right, begin with the soupspoon on the outside, then the fish knife, ending with the dinner knife closest to the plate. Place the cutlery on the table so that the bottoms of all the pieces align. The dessert cutlery can go above the plate or you may follow my example and wait until dessert is served to place it on the table.

It is customary to provide salt and pepper at each table, since your taste in seasoning may not be that of your guests. (However, I must say I consider it rude when guests immediately throw salt on their food without tasting it.)

At my private dinners, I do not put ashtrays on the table until after dessert has been served. If guests want to smoke at this point, it is polite to ask permission of their table companions first. (If anyone is dying for a smoke before this, you could ask him or her to light up in another room or outdoors.)

Glasses

The white wine glass is generally placed half an inch above the top of the knife. The red wine glass goes one inch to the left and at a slight angle from the white wine glass. The water glass sits at a point between and above the red and white wine glasses, so that they form a triangle.

Tables and Chairs

Make sure not to put too many people at the table, making everyone uncomfortable. When you arrange the chairs, give each guest five to six inches of space on each side. Leave enough room around the table or between tables so that you or your staff can pass between them or, if it is a buffet, so that your guests can move freely. If someone brings an unexpected guest, make the best of the situation and squeeze him or her in, using a folding chair if necessary.

Of course, your seating depends on the furniture in your dining room. I personally prefer round tables, which make conversation among guests easier than do long tables. You might take this factor into consideration if you are renting tables for a large party.

Lighting

Candles or dim light provide the best lighting for evening entertaining. Candlelight immediately creates a special atmosphere, and it flatters everyone's looks. You want to achieve a level that makes the room look romantic and glowing but not so dim that you cannot see the food.

Dripless candles in safe holders work best. Cheap candles will not last as long and will drip on the tablecloth. By the way, if you should get candle wax on your tablecloth, I have found an excellent method to remove it. Scrape off as much wax as you can, then put a white paper towel or tissue paper over the wax. Go over it with a warm iron, and the paper will absorb the wax. Repeat until all the wax is gone.

Flowers

Flowers are the jewelry of nature, one of the greatest delights God has given us. They have always been among the most important enhancements of my home. When I had little money to spend, I never stopped buying flowers; I could not live without the color, life, and festivity they bring into a space. Even a few daisies purchased at the supermarket can transform the atmosphere of a room.

If you buy flowers often, it helps to get to know a good florist. Talk to him each time until you get acquainted and bribe him with goodies. A good florist will give you plenty of advice about arranging and keeping flowers and might even call occasionally to offer you special prices. Tell the florist your color scheme and the style of your house—you might even consider having him come to your home—so he will be able to judge which arrangements will suit your style.

There are several things you can do to make flowers last a long time. First of all, the vase or container you plan to arrange them in must be scrupulously clean, since the bacteria that grow in the water are what kills the flowers. Wash nonmetal containers with a light solution of bleach (2 quarts of water with 1 tablespoon Clorox). Do not use bleach on metal containers, since it will discolor them. As soon as you unwrap your fresh flowers, put them in a container, up to their necks (where the bud starts) in warm water. Cut the flower stems with a sharp knife or scissors under water. The idea is to get as much water up the stem as possible. If you cut the stem out of water, air will travel into the stem and prevent the water from going all the way up. When you are ready to arrange the flowers, put some Floralife in the container or change the water every second day. This keeps down the bacteria. Forget about adding aspirin, sugar, pennies, or any other folk remedies.

I avoid using the florist's foam called Oasis for arrangements because flowers will not last as long in this medium. Oasis clogs the stem and prevents water from traveling up to the blossom. This is particularly true of roses, I have found. If you need a base of some kind to hold your flowers, try a frog or glass marbles. If you have a flower with a long stem and a large head, use florist's wire to reinforce the stem. It will hold the flower erect, allowing the water to reach the blossom and consequently prolong its life.

If your flowers look wilted and you want to revive them, dip the stems into boiling water for one minute. Then cut the stem with a sharp knife or scissors under water. Wash out the container and add fresh water. When the heads of roses droop, they can be revived by wrapping them in newspaper and floating them in a sinkful of water overnight. I don't know why this works, but it does.

In my home, I like to use flowers that are in season or slightly ahead of the season. Nothing can brighten a gray January or February day like a few spring flowers. I also like to use flowers to adorn my gifts; they make the package twice as special.

When it comes to choosing flowers, one or two blossoms in a small vial, or an

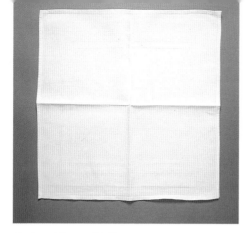

The lotus blossom fold begins with a lightly starched square of linen or cotton, preferably 20 inches square. (Spray starch works well, but it may take some experimentation to achieve the right amount of starch, since an overly starched napkin will not fold properly.)

Fold each corner of the napkin into the center

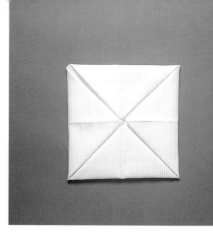

Again fold each corner into the center

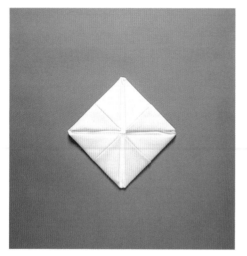

Turn the napkin over and again fold the corners into the center

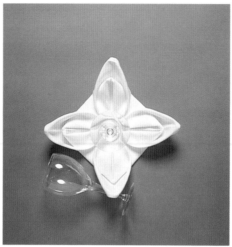

Firmly press the head of a wineglass into the center of the napkin and pull up each point from underneath

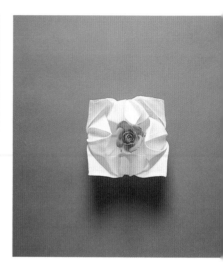

Replace the wineglass with a fresh flower in a small vase or vial no taller than the napkin

Ikebana (Japanese-style) arrangement, can be more dramatic than a dozen flowers in a crystal vase. Experiment with unusual types of containers for flowers, such as wine or medicine bottles, spice bottles, copper molds, crockery, casseroles, tankards, baskets—even hollowed-out vegetables and fruit, such as a gourd, squash, or pear.

As I always believe in learning from the best, I have studied books and magazine articles by experts about flower arranging. The one I like best is Denise Otis and Ronaldo Maia's *Decorating with Flowers* (New York: Abrams, 1978), which I consult often for new ideas. I also keep a file of articles clipped from magazines. I now have a florist as a member of my staff, but I still like to offer my own suggestions for imaginative arrangements.

WINES AND BAR

ॐ

J UST as you want your dinner to run smoothly, you also want to organize your refreshment service so well that you will not have to give it a second thought once your party has started.

If you are entertaining fewer than twelve guests, you should not need to hire a bartender; you might ask your spouse or a friend to help out with the drinks or set up a self-service bar. With a guest list over twelve, it is probably worth your while to hire a bartender, who can provide the smoothest, most hassle-free drink service.

When entertaining, the general rule is to allow for two and a half drinks per person. Of course, some will drink more, but some will also nurse one drink all evening or simply drink soda. A fifth of liquor provides twenty drinks, and a bottle of wine or champagne gives five to seven glasses per bottle.

If you are setting up a full bar, the following liquors (in order of usual preferences)

Guests enjoy a cocktail before dinner

A waiter offers guests a Kir Royale aperitif

11

are recommended: vodka, scotch, gin, rye, bourbon, and rum. Since the last three liquors are less popular, you need fewer bottles of them for large parties. You should also have a bottle of vermouth on hand for mixing martinis. (My bartender, Kevin, hints that if you do not have vermouth, you can make a creditable martini by substituting a few drops of white wine.) An alternative to the full bar is the simple full bar, which offers vodka, scotch, and gin.

It is always preferable to buy too much than to underestimate and chance running out halfway into the party. Most liquor stores will allow you to return unopened bottles when you place a big order, provided state law allows it.

Just as you buy the freshest and best ingredients for your dinner menu, you will want to buy good brands of liquor. You can never be sure of the quality of store brands, and in this area, guests can immediately get the impression that you have skimped.

Other standard bar items include fruit such as olives, onions, lemons, and limes, a small cutting board and knife, and Bloody Mary mix, orange juice, and grapefruit juice. Such garnishes as maraschino cherries and orange slices are optional.

Wines

With your liquor, you should also provide wine, which many guests these days favor over spirits. My bartender recommends that you serve only one kind of white wine, choosing it on the basis of your budget. If you are serving champagne, select on this basis as well, figuring five to seven glasses per bottle. If you plan to have red wine for the bar, order one-quarter the amount of white wine. (That is, if you order a case of white wine, order three bottles of red.)

I always offer my guests a Kir Royale when they enter. To make this, simply put a couple of drops of Crème de Cassis or Framboise brandy in the bottom of a tulip or flute champagne glass, then fill the glass with champagne. It turns a lovely pale pink color and sets the tone for an elegant evening. One bottle of the Cassis or Framboise will probably last for several parties.

Another alternative to the full bar, increasingly popular, is the white bar, which provides wine, champagne, vodka, and vermouth with seltzer and tonic. While somewhat limited, it still gives several choices to guests, most of whom will happily accept whatever they are offered.

Soda and Beer

I have found that mixers are often the first item to run out at a party. If you order plenty of soda from the liquor store, it will generally take back any unopened bottles along with any liquor you might return. In addition to soda, you will need tonic water, cola, both diet and regular, a lemon-lime soda or ginger ale, and plenty of sparkling mineral water.

If you know you are serving a crowd that likes beer, allow at least one and a half cans per person, providing a choice of regular and light beers. If it is not a beer-drinking group, the general rule is half a case of beer for every case of wine you order.

Ice

For ten to fifteen people, you will need two five-pound bags of ice for drinks and two five-pound bags for chilling beer and wine in a cooler or washtub. Many liquor stores will provide ice free of charge with a large party order; remember to ask when you place your order.

For a larger party, you might consider calling a professional ice company to deliver a twenty-pound tin or forty-pound bag of ice. A party of fifty or sixty, for example, calls for two forty-pound bags.

Glassware

For a party of over twelve guests, I recommend renting glassware. It saves a lot of work—no glasses to wash—and a lot of wear and tear on your own barware. (I do not use plastic cups, for several reasons: they are unpleasant to use; they are ecologically unsound; and, in the long run, they don't save all that much money.) Order six- to eight-ounce stemmed glasses for mixed drinks as well as for wine to simplify your glassware needs. Allow two and a half glasses per person, as people often put their drinks down and lose track of them. When ordering champagne glasses, be sure to specify either tulip- or flute-shaped glasses, which, unlike the coupe glass, preserve the fizz, and ask for as many glasses as guests plus 10 percent of the guest count.

Other essential items for a party include cocktail napkins, two and a half per person, and matches and ashtrays. The bar should be equipped with a stirrer, a pitcher of water, a corkscrew, and a couple of large white napkins, used primarily for opening champagne.

This brings up the proper way to open champagne: remove the foil and place the bar napkin over the cork before loosening the wire collar. When the collar is loose, twist the cork gently with one hand to ease it out under the napkin. If the cork happens to fly out suddenly, the napkin will prevent it from taking off. Prying the cork out with your thumbs without using a napkin is very dangerous; it can cause injury if the cork flies into someone's eye.

NOTE ON THE RECIPES

BEFORE you start reading and cooking my recipes, I would like you to know about some of the ingredients I use, so that you will get the results I get.

I use strictly unsalted butter, as I prefer to add my own salt when needed, and because it freezes better.

Most of the herbs specified in the recipes are dried (Spice Islands is a good brand), since fresh herbs are not available everywhere. If you use fresh herbs instead, the rule of thumb is to use twice the amount specified for dried.

When I need chicken or beef broth, I use Campbell's canned broths, which are condensed or double strength and come in 10½-ounce cans. They can be watered down if necessary or kept full strength for some sauces. Keep in mind that these products contain a large amount of salt, so adjust your seasoning accordingly. If you need to watch your salt intake, Campbell's now makes a lower-sodium broth.

Since I use less salt than most people I rarely give exact amounts, so I usually instruct readers to add until it suits their taste. When using pepper I always use freshly ground black peppercorns.

I also use a seasoning called Maggi, which comes from Germany, in some of my salad dressings. Most supermarkets carry it in the condiments or seasonings sections. Spike Vegetable Seasoning can be found in most health-food stores.

HORS D'OEUVRES

A S I mentioned earlier, I am not fond of making hors d'oeuvres. In the first place, by the time I have made six or eight little hors d'oeuvres, I could have been well into preparing a six-course meal. Because of the disproportionate amount of labor involved, I almost never accept cocktail and hors d'oeuvres parties for business. Also, since I generally serve a six-course meal, I want my guests to enjoy each course, which is difficult if they are full before they come to the table. Still, there are times when hors d'oeuvres come in handy—for example, when waiting for an out-of-town guest prolongs the cocktail hour. Under such circumstances, I would rather make a few canapés than have people fall over from hunger or inebriation.

When I make hors d'oeuvres, I always serve them small enough to be eaten in one bite or easy to cut or dip. Few things are more embarrassing than biting into an hors d'oeuvre and having the rest of it come apart all over one's clothes, the furniture, and the carpet.

The hors d'oeuvres I have included here are all easy to make and very delicious. Many of them may also be served as a light meal, for lunch, or as a first course at dinner.

Cheese Rolls (page 16)

CHEESE ROLLS

OTHER than for hors d'oeuvres, I make these rolls when I'm planning to go on a picnic. They can be made a day before and kept wrapped in plastic in the refrigerator overnight. If you want a crunchy, fresh texture to the bread, I suggest that you make the cheese mixture the day before and wait until the day you are serving to stuff it into the French bread, allowing it to rest for an hour or two before you slice it.

½ pound imported Swiss cheese (Emmenthal), grated
¼ pound Parmesan cheese, grated
½ cup (1 stick) butter, softened
Heavy cream, about ¼ cup
½ cup raw, shelled, unsalted pistachio nuts, chopped
1 loaf French bread, preferably 1½" in diameter

In a food processor, blend the Swiss cheese, Parmesan cheese, and butter, adding enough cream to make a thick paste. Add pistachio nuts and process briefly.

Trim the ends off a loaf of French bread. Cut in half across and hollow out the soft inside with a long spoon or knife. Stuff the bread shells with the cheese and nut mixture. Chill the rolls for several hours.

Before serving, remove rolls from refrigerator and let sit at room temperature for an hour or two. Cut them crosswise into thin slices.

HOT BRIE WITH ALMONDS

THIS is, without a doubt, one of the easiest hors d'oeuvres imaginable to make, and, to put the icing on the cake, everyone loves it.

You may cut the top off the Brie ahead of time, sprinkle the almonds on, and keep it covered in the refrigerator until you are ready to pop it in the oven.

1 whole round of ripe Brie, 1 or 2 pounds
½ cup blanched, sliced almonds

Preheat oven to 375° F.

Cut the top rind off the Brie with a serrated knife. Place the cheese in a round, shallow ovenproof dish, such as a ceramic quiche dish or a Pyrex pie plate. Sprinkle the top with the almonds.

Bake for 15 to 20 minutes, or until cheese is hot and almonds are lightly browned. Serve with thin slices of French bread.

THIS chicken liver pâté is not only one of the easiest to make, but its apples and Calvados give it a truly wonderful taste. The apple flavor keeps the chicken liver taste from being overpowering.

This recipe can be made several days ahead of time and kept in the refrigerator. In fact, it is best made at least the day before, giving the flavors a chance to mingle.

I serve this with wheat thins or with thin slices of apple, such as Granny Smith.

2 tablespoons vegetable oil
2 tablespoons butter
1 medium onion, coarsely chopped
1 Granny Smith apple, peeled, cored, and chopped
½ teaspoon thyme
Salt and pepper to taste
1 pound chicken livers, all fat removed
¼ cup Calvados (French apple brandy)
½ cup (1 stick) butter, at room temperature

Heat the vegetable oil and the 2 tablespoons butter in a heavy sauté pan. Add the onion, apple, thyme, salt, and pepper and sauté until lightly browned. Cover the pan and simmer until the apple is soft, about 3 minutes. With a slotted spoon, remove this mixture from the pan and reserve.

In the same pan, adding a little more butter if necessary, sauté the chicken livers, being careful not to overcook them. (The livers should still be pink inside.)

Warm the Calvados, carefully set aflame, and pour over the chicken livers. When the flame has died out, add the onion-apple mixture, stir well, and let cool.

Put this mixture in the food processor, add the ½ cup butter, a tablespoon at a time, and puree until smooth. Put into a dish or decorative tureen and refrigerate for several hours before serving.

GUACAMOLE

SERVES: 8

H ERE is one hors d'oeuvre even I can truly appreciate. When I was the executive chef of *Gourmet* magazine, this recipe was almost a staple before lunch, since everybody loved it so much.

Unfortunately, guacamole cannot be made too far ahead of time, even when you take the precaution of adding the avocado pits to the finished dish to keep it from discoloring. One way to prepare ahead is to cut the onion, tomato, cilantro, and pepper and keep them covered in the refrigerator. Then all you have to do is add the avocados, lime juice, salt, and pepper about one hour before serving. Put the pits in, cover with plastic wrap, and refrigerate.

I find the California avocados—the ones with rough, dark skin—creamier and prefer them to the green-skinned Florida variety, which seem more watery.

Also—and this is true of all recipes—try the finished guacamole and experiment with the proportions: whether you like more or less hot pepper, lime juice, and so on. It is all a matter of taste—and yours is the best guide.

CAUTION: When you handle the jalapeño pepper, wear rubber gloves and do not touch any part of your face, especially the eyes, while handling it, as it can make your skin or eyes burn.

> *2 ripe California (Hess) avocados*
> *Juice of 1 lime*
> *½ Bermuda onion, finely chopped*
> *1 ripe tomato, chopped*
> *1 tablespoon chopped fresh cilantro (coriander)*
> *1 fresh jalapeño pepper, seeded and finely chopped*
> *Salt and pepper to taste*

Cut the avocados in half and peel them. Remove the pits and reserve (see above).

In a bowl, break the avocados into small pieces with a fork, then add the rest of the ingredients. Combine well. Taste and adjust the ingredients to suit your liking.

CAMEMBERT GLACÉ

SERVES: 12

I used to serve this molded cheese when I worked for Jacqueline Kennedy, from whom I got the recipe. It was rumored that she got it from the Duchess of Windsor.

Whatever the true story is, the recipe must be well over twenty years old, and it is a delectable cheese dish. It proves that some good things just keep getting better.

Make sure you get a good Camembert, ripe but not so ripe that it smells like ammonia. There is a fine line between ripe and spoiled. Pick a cheese that has the same give when touched in the middle as the bottommost part of your thumb. The riper the Camembert, the stronger the flavor.

Serve with fresh pear slices or whole wheat or water crackers.

This dish can be made a day or two ahead.

> *1 pound very ripe Camembert cheese (see above)*
> *2 cups dry white wine*

2 cups (1 pound) butter, softened
Toasted bread crumbs for garnish

Remove and discard the white rind of the Camembert. Cut cheese into small pieces. Place cheese in a bowl. Pour white wine over it to cover. Cover bowl with plastic wrap and let stand overnight.

The next day, discard the wine. Put the cheese through a sieve and thoroughly mix with the softened butter, preferably using an electric mixer or a food processor.

Put cheese mixture in a plain, round, 2-cup mold that has been lined with waxed paper or clear plastic wrap. Cover and refrigerate until firm.

Remove from refrigerator one hour before serving. Unmold and garnish with toasted bread crumbs.

LORNA'S STUFFED GRAPE LEAVES

YIELD: ABOUT 80

ONE of the joys in being invited to someone else's house is that you discover wonderful new dishes. Several years ago, at a Thanksgiving dinner in the country, Lorna served these stuffed grape leaves, without a doubt the best I have ever eaten. Lorna shared the recipe with me and I showed her husband, Patrick, how to carve the turkey more easily.

They are truly worth the effort, especially since you can make them a day or two ahead. In fact, they are best made at least five hours before serving. I always make an extra batch and have some for lunch the next day.

NOTE: I recommend Orlando brand grape leaves.

2/3 cup seedless currants soaked in
2 cups white wine
1-quart jar grape leaves (80 per jar)
2 bunches scallions, finely chopped
2 tablespoons finely chopped fresh parsley
1½ cups olive oil, total
1½ cups uncooked short-grain brown rice
2 tablespoons finely chopped fresh dill
¾ cup pine nuts
Salt and pepper to taste
Juice of 4 lemons, about 1 cup
3 cups condensed beef broth
2 cups water

Soak currants in wine for about 30 minutes.

Remove grape leaves from jar, put them in a colander in the sink, and pour boiling water over them. Carefully cut off stems and discard. Pat each leaf dry and place, shiny surface down, on paper towels.

In a skillet, sauté scallions and parsley in 4 teaspoons of the olive oil. Add the rice, dill, pine nuts, currants with the wine, salt, and pepper. Bring to a boil, then reduce heat. Cover and simmer for 20 minutes. If liquid evaporates, add half a cup water. Rice will not be fully cooked at the end of this time. Set aside and cool.

When rice mixture is cool, place 1 teaspoon of it in the center of each leaf. Fold stem side of leaf over to cover filling. Fold up sides of leaf and roll carefully to form a cylinder about 2 inches long.

In a heavy pot, arrange the stuffed grape leaves, seam side down, in layers. Sprinkle each layer with lemon juice and 2 teaspoons of the olive oil. Pour the beef broth, the 2 cups water, and the remaining olive oil and lemon juice over them.

Place a plate on top to weight down the grape-leaf cylinders and simmer over very low heat for 40 to 50 minutes. Cool for a few hours before serving.

At serving time, pour off excess moisture and arrange on a platter.

FIRST COURSES

THE only time I serve asparagus is when it is in season in New York—April, May, and June. Then I have it in every way, shape, and form imaginable. This particular vinaigrette is also wonderful over cooked artichokes.

I always peel my asparagus, to a point half an inch below the tip, before cooking, as it tastes sweeter and cooks more quickly. I cook it al dente, leaving it somewhat crunchy.

You may cook the asparagus and make the vinaigrette sauce earlier in the day, but do not combine the two until just before serving time.

2 pounds asparagus, the tough ends cut off, peeled, and washed
1/2 cup vegetable oil
2 tablespoons olive or hazelnut oil
3 tablespoons cider vinegar
1 teaspoon honey
1 tablespoon Dijon or Pommery mustard
2 hard-boiled eggs, put through a coarse strainer or finely chopped
2 tablespoons finely chopped fresh parsley
2 tablespoons chopped pimiento

Steam the asparagus until it is tender but still crisp.

Put the oils, vinegar, honey, and mustard in a blender and blend well. Pour into a bowl and add eggs, parsley, and pimiento and combine well with a fork. Pour dressing over cooked and cooled asparagus.

ASPARAGUS VINAIGRETTE

SERVES: 4 TO 6

HOT STILTON CHEESE SOUFFLÉ

SERVES: 6

NOT only is this an excellent first course, it is also very good served as a cheese course before or after dessert. For that purpose, put a few slices of pears in the bottom of the soufflé dish before you pour the soufflé mixture in.

You can make the cheese mixture ahead of time and then reheat it before adding the egg yolks.

Individual soufflés made in small ramekins rather than one large soufflé look very lovely.

NOTE: When making this in individual dishes, bake in a 400° F. oven for about 15 minutes, or until they have risen and are lightly browned on top.

4 tablespoons butter
4 tablespoons flour
1¹/₂ cups milk, heated
2 cups crumbled Stilton cheese, about 1 pound
1 teaspoon salt
6 eggs, separated

Preheat oven to 375° F.

Melt the butter in a saucepan. Stir in the flour and blend well with a wooden spoon. Add the hot milk, stirring with a wire whisk constantly until it comes to a boil. Add the cheese and stir until melted. Add salt and remove from heat.

Add the egg yolks one by one, stirring well after each addition.

Beat the egg whites until stiff, then fold them carefully into the hot cheese mixture. Pour into a generously buttered 2-quart soufflé dish and bake for about 30 minutes.

Serve immediately.

T HIS is great for a summer buffet or as a first course served with dilled cucumbers and dark bread. It may also be served as an hors d'oeuvre, with the salmon strips thinly sliced and placed on dark bread and topped with a little mustard sauce and a sprig of dill.

This recipe must be made a few days ahead of time, so you need to remember to plan accordingly. It also helps to have a great fish dealer, as this recipe requires the freshest and best fish possible. When ordering the salmon, ask for the center section (in order for the fish to cure evenly) with the backbone, as well as all the other little bones, removed. When you get it, run your hand over the fish; if you feel any small bones, remove them. I reserve an eyebrow tweezer for this purpose, as it works best.

Don't let these directions dissuade you from making this dish; it is truly worth the planning and effort.

> 2-pound piece of salmon (see above)
> 4 tablespoons sugar
> 3 tablespoons coarse salt (kosher)
> 1 tablespoon coarsely ground black pepper
> 1 large bunch fresh dill

Place the fish skin side down on your counter. Mix the sugar, salt, and pepper together in a small bowl. Rub the mixture well into the fish. Wash and dry the dill and place it on the fish. Fold the fish over the dill like a sandwich.

Place the fish in a plastic bag and seal the bag. Put it on a platter in the refrigerator and weight it down. (Large cans of food are ideal for this purpose.) Refrigerate for at least 24 hours or, better yet, up to 4 days. Remove the weights and turn the fish about every 8 to 10 hours during that time.

When salmon is cured, or ready, remove it from the bag, scrape away the dill and seasoning, and pat the fish dry with paper towels. Place skin side down on a carving board and slice the salmon, as thinly as possible, on the diagonal, separating each slice from the skin. Serve with Mustard Dill Sauce and thin slices of dark bread.

MUSTARD DILL SAUCE:
> 3 tablespoons Dijon style or Pommery mustard
> $1/_3$ cup vegetable oil
> 2 tablespoons cider vinegar
> 1 tablespoon sugar
> $1/_4$ teaspoon salt
> 1 tablespoon finely chopped fresh dill

Combine all ingredients thoroughly.

GRAVLAX WITH MUSTARD DILL SAUCE

SERVES: 8 AS A FIRST COURSE
16 AS AN HORS D'OEUVRE

SEAFOOD SAUSAGE WITH HERB BEURRE BLANC

SERVES: 6 TO 8

THIS is a version of my shrimp and scallop mousse. It is a wonderful first course, and the sausage by itself, without the sauce, makes a nice hors d'oeuvre. You can make this mixture several hours ahead of time, keeping it in a covered glass bowl in the refrigerator or already shaped and wrapped in Saran Wrap (see CAUTION), and then take it out and poach it at the last minute. It only takes 15 minutes, and it is best not reheated.

In the process of making this dish many times, I have learned in cooking the sausage that it is essential not to let the water come to a rolling boil but to keep it just at boiling point and also never to cover the pot. Both of these procedures will make the seafood mixture break down and either take on a grainy texture or fall apart, making it difficult or impossible to slice the sausage.

CAUTION: Saran Wrap is the only brand of plastic wrap, I have found, that can be boiled.

> 1 pound medium shrimp, shelled and cleaned
> 1 pound scallops, cleaned
> 2 whole eggs
> 2 cups light cream
> 1/2 teaspoon salt
> Pepper to taste

Reserve 4 shrimp. Put scallops and remaining shrimp in a food processor. Add eggs and process for 20 seconds. Continue processing while adding cream in a thin stream. Season with salt and pepper. Process another 20 seconds to combine seasonings with seafood.

Chop reserved 4 shrimp by hand and fold into seafood mixture by hand.

Take 4 sheets of Saran Wrap, each 12 inches long. Divide seafood mixture evenly among the sheets and place at one end of each sheet. Roll mixture up in the Saran Wrap, sausage style. Twist the sides to close or tie each side tightly with a piece of kitchen twine, then wrap each roll in aluminum foil for added security.

Fill a large sauté pan with water and heat it. When it comes to a boil, lower the heat and keep the water at a low simmer. Put the seafood sausages in the pan, uncovered, and poach for 15 minutes, turning them once. Make sure the water does not get too hot, which might make the sausages burst.

In the meantime, make Herb Beurre Blanc.

At serving time, remove aluminum foil and Saran Wrap. Cut sausages in slices. Arrange on a platter and pour Herb Beurre Blanc over the slices.

HERB BEURRE BLANC:
> 1/2 cup white wine
> 1/2 cup white wine vinegar
> 3 tablespoons chopped shallots
> 1 cup (2 sticks) butter, cut into tablespoon-size pieces
> 1 tablespoon chopped fresh dill
> 1 tablespoon chopped fresh tarragon

1 tablespoon chopped fresh chives
1 tablespoon chopped fresh parsley

Put the white wine, vinegar, and shallots in a saucepan. Bring to a boil and reduce by half. Add the butter, little by little, stirring with a whisk until well combined, making sure it does not come to a boil. Finally, add the dill, tarragon, chives, and parsley. Combine well.

I rarely serve pasta in my dining room because we generally have a large group, and pasta does not lend itself well to large numbers. However, I often made this recipe for the executive dining room at *Gourmet* magazine for lunch, served with an arugula salad. For entertaining at home, it makes a wonderful first course. It takes very little time, but it must be served immediately. Assembling all the ingredients ahead of time will help it go smoothly.

NOTE: If Mascarpone cheese is unavailable, sour cream may be substituted.

1 pound fettuccine, preferably fresh
¹/₂ cup (1 stick) butter
¹/₂ cup Mascarpone cheese
1 cup heavy cream
Salt and pepper to taste
¹/₂ cup Parmesan cheese, freshly grated
¹/₂ pound smoked salmon, cut into narrow strips
1 bunch fresh chives, snipped
6 tablespoons fresh or canned salmon caviar
¹/₄ cup Parmesan cheese, freshly grated

Heat 4 quarts of water for cooking the pasta while preparing the sauce.

In a large sauté pan, melt the butter. Add the Mascarpone cheese, heavy cream, salt, pepper, and ¹/₂ cup Parmesan cheese. Combine with a whisk and heat gently on low heat to the point just before it comes to a boil. Add the smoked salmon and most of the chives, reserving about a tablespoon for garnish.

Cook the fettuccine al dente, drain, and toss with the sauce to combine well. Divide the pasta onto 6 plates. Place a tablespoon of fresh salmon caviar on top of each serving and sprinkle the Parmesan cheese and chives over. Serve immediately.

PASTA WITH SMOKED SALMON AND CAVIAR

SERVES: 6 AS A FIRST COURSE
4 AS A LUNCHEON

In order to have fresh herbs on hand at all times, Annemarie grows her favorites in her greenhouse. This selection includes (clockwise from top) *purple basil, tarragon, green basil, sage, miniature basil, thyme, flat or Italian parsley, and oregano*

Seafood Mélange in Saffron Sauce (page 28)

OPPOSITE: *Pasta with Smoked Salmon and Caviar (page 25)*

27

SEAFOOD MÉLANGE IN SAFFRON SAUCE

SERVES: 10

THIS is a very elegant first course for a special occasion. It also makes a lovely luncheon dish. To top it off, it is really very easily prepared.

When it comes to puff pastry, my philosophy "if others can make it as well as you, let them" enters in. Unless you really enjoy making it yourself, use the Pepperidge Farm puff pastry, which is excellent. Make sure you follow the package directions for defrosting, as it generally comes frozen.

I like to use an oval cutout shape, but you may use whatever shape you like, using a cookie cutter or any other guide you choose.

The sauce can be made several hours in advance or, for that matter, the day before, and kept in the refrigerator until you are ready to cook. Then all you have to do at serving time is add the seafood and let it come to a boil, which is sufficient to cook the fish. If you overcook the seafood, it will toughen.

1 package frozen puff pastry sheets (Pepperidge Farm brand works well), defrosted according to the package's directions
1 pound sea scallops, cleaned and cut in half horizontally
1 pound medium-size shrimp, shelled, cleaned, and cut in half horizontally
1 pound cooked lobster meat, cut into 1/2-inch pieces
10 oysters, fresh out of the shell in their own juice
4 tablespoons (1/2 stick) butter
4 tablespoons flour
2 cups shrimp stock (page 112)
1/2 teaspoon saffron threads
Salt and pepper to taste
1/2 cup heavy cream

GARNISH:
Pink peppercorns
Chopped fresh chives

Cut out 10 pastry shells from the pastry sheets in whatever shape you desire. Put them on a cookie sheet and bake them according to package directions. Keep warm or, if you have made them earlier, heat them just before serving.

Clean all your seafood well, making sure there are no pieces of shell left.

Melt the butter in a large sauté pan. Add the flour and combine well. Add the shrimp stock, saffron threads, salt, and pepper. Combine well, whisking the sauce until it comes to a boil, then simmer for about 10 minutes.

Add the heavy cream and return sauce to the boil, then add the scallops and shrimp. Reduce heat to low and stir the mixture constantly. When it comes back to a boil, add the oysters with their juice and the cooked lobster meat. Heat through until just before it boils.

To serve, put a split pastry shell on the plate and place some of the seafood mixture in the bottom half, making sure that there is some of each kind of shellfish. Sprinkle a few pink peppercorns and chopped chives on top. Cover with the top half of the pastry shell. Serve immediately.

SINCE salmon is one of my favorite fish, I try to prepare it many different ways. I love the colors and texture of this sauce with the salmon.

2 pounds salmon fillets, skinned and boned
Salt and pepper to taste
1 tablespoon sesame seeds
¼ cup fish stock (page 112), using the salmon skin and bones

Preheat oven to 375° F.

Cut the salmon into 6 pieces and rub each with salt and pepper and the sesame seeds. Put the salmon in an ovenproof dish (a ceramic quiche dish or a Pyrex pie pan) and pour the ¼ cup fish stock into it. Put in the oven and bake for 10 to 15 minutes until done.

In the meantime, make the Oriental Watercress Sauce.

ORIENTAL WATERCRESS SAUCE:
¾ cup fish stock
2 tablespoons soy sauce
2 tablespoons hoisin sauce
1 tablespoon Oriental sesame oil
½ cup condensed chicken broth
1 teaspoon cornstarch, mixed with a little water
1 can water chestnuts, cut into strips
1 bunch watercress, washed

In a saucepan, reduce the ¾ cup fish stock by half. Add the soy sauce, hoisin sauce, sesame oil, and chicken broth. Bring to a boil and simmer for 5 minutes. Add the cornstarch mixture and bring to a boil again. Add water chestnuts and watercress. Stir and pour over the salmon.

SALMON WITH ORIENTAL WATERCRESS SAUCE

SERVES: 6

THIS is probably the most popular first course in my dining room, and rightfully so: it not only looks fabulous, it also tastes great.

Fresh phyllo is much easier to work with than frozen. The best place to get fresh phyllo dough is an Indian or Greek food shop. Since phyllo is a paper-thin dough, it tends to dry out very quickly, so you need to work fast. Many food writers recommend placing a moist towel over the dough, but I find it makes the dough sticky and even tougher to work with. I just unpack it at the last minute, making sure that all my other ingredients are lined up and ready to use, and go. Any leftover phyllo can be rewrapped in plastic wrap and kept in the refrigerator for a week or two.

Choose a salmon fillet with no skin or bones. If you should find any small bones, use an eyebrow tweezer to remove them.

I start my oven temperature at 375° F. and if the phyllo does not brown after 5

SALMON IN PHYLLO

SERVES: 8

minutes, I raise the temperature to 400°, as I don't want to overcook the salmon by keeping it in too long.

2 pounds salmon fillet, skinned and boned and cut into 8 portions
Juice of 1 lemon
1 tablespoon chopped fresh dill
Salt and pepper to taste
8 sheets phyllo dough
4 tablespoons (1/2 stick) butter, melted
1 teaspoon Dijon or coarse-grain mustard
1 egg yolk
1 tablespoon heavy cream
Fresh dill for garnish

Marinate salmon in lemon juice and dill for about 20 minutes. Season with salt and pepper, rubbing in well. (This can be done several hours ahead of time.)

Preheat oven to 375° F.

Take a sheet of phyllo dough. Combine melted butter and mustard and brush lightly over the phyllo. Put a strip of salmon at the long end of the dough. Fold phyllo over salmon and roll up. Two inches from the end of the sheet, tuck the sides in toward the middle. Finish rolling and place roll on buttered baking sheet, seam side down. Repeat with remaining salmon strips. This step can be done an hour ahead and the salmon refrigerated.

Combine egg yolk and heavy cream and brush the pastry with this egg wash. Bake until phyllo is puffed and browned, about 5 to 7 minutes (see above). At this point the salmon as well as the pastry will be cooked.

At serving time, put pastry on a heated plate. Put a sprig of dill on top. Pour Shrimp (or Lobster) Sauce around it. Serve immediately.

SHRIMP (OR LOBSTER) SAUCE
4 tablespoons butter
3 tablespoons flour
2 cups shrimp (or lobster) stock (page 112)
1/2 cup heavy cream
Salt and pepper to taste

Melt butter, add flour, and blend well. Add remaining ingredients, combine well, and cook until thickened, stirring constantly until it comes to a boil. Simmer 3 more minutes, stirring constantly.

SOUPS

S OUPS are among my favorite dishes, whether as a first course or a main meal. One of my more successful parties, which I gave to celebrate the publication of my second cookbook, was a soup party, where everyone had a great time. I offered four different soups: Butternut Squash and Apple, Black Bean, Chicken Noodle, and Hot and Sour. Served with different kinds of breads, they made a most satisfying meal. Since I was able to make the soups ahead of time, I could devote myself to my guests instead of cooking.

Unless otherwise specified, most soups can be made at least one day before serving them. However. wait until just before serving time to add any cream that the recipe calls for.

T HIS velvety soup is easy to make, as long as it is not allowed to curdle. It is just as delicious hot as it is cold. If you serve it cold, make it a day ahead.

2 cans condensed chicken broth
1 cup water
1 cup finely chopped cooked chicken
1 tablespoon curry powder
4 egg yolks
2 cups heavy cream
Salt and pepper to taste
1 tablespoon chopped pimiento (or 1 tablespoon chopped truffles) for garnish

SENEGALESE SOUP

SERVES: 6

Combine the chicken broth and water in a large saucepan and bring to a boil. Add the chicken meat and curry powder.

In a bowl, add the egg yolks to the heavy cream and mix well. Add this to the soup, stirring constantly over low heat until the soup is just thickened, being careful not to bring to a boil, as the eggs will curdle.

Season to taste and serve or chill. Before serving, garnish with either a little chopped pimiento or truffle on top of each serving.

ROASTED EGGPLANT SOUP

SERVES: 6

THIS is another recipe that originated in the dining room of *Gourmet* magazine. It is very unusual without being too esoteric. It is simple to make, can be made several days ahead of time, and freezes well.

3 pounds eggplant, unpeeled, cut into cubes
¼ cup olive oil
1 teaspoon salt
1 teaspoon pepper
¼ cup olive oil
1½ cups chopped onion
3 garlic cloves, minced
1 bay leaf
½ teaspoon thyme
¼ teaspoon sage
5 cans condensed chicken broth
2½ cups water
2 tablespoons Marsala, optional

GARNISH:
Chopped fresh chives
Crème fraîche (page 116)

Preheat oven to 450° F.

In a jelly roll pan, toss the eggplant cubes with ¼ cup of the olive oil, salt, and pepper. Roast in the oven, stirring occasionally, for 15 minutes.

In a heavy saucepan, cook the onion, garlic, and the bay leaf in ¼ cup oil over moderately low heat, stirring occasionally until the onion is softened. Add the eggplant, thyme, and sage and cook the mixture, stirring occasionally, for 5 minutes. Add the broth, water, and Marsala, if desired, and simmer, covered, for 10 minutes.

Discard the bay leaf, cool the soup, then puree it in a blender 2 cups at a time, transferring the puree to the saucepan. Reheat at serving time and garnish with crème fraîche and chives.

TOMATO SOUP WITH BASIL

SERVES: 16

THE only time I make this soup is when New Jersey Beefsteak tomatoes are in season, from the end of July until late September, when basil is also plentiful. On occasion, when friends have brought tomatoes to me in bushels, I have made large batches of soup and then frozen it, so as to give me a taste of summer bounty in the depths of winter. As long as you have a good freezer, the taste remains almost the same.

The best way to peel the tomatoes is to immerse them in a 3-quart pot of boiling water for about 20 seconds, depending on the ripeness of the tomatoes (less ripe tomatoes take a bit longer). Remove them with a slotted spoon and peel with a paring knife.

2 cups sliced leeks, trimmed of their coarse green ends

1 cup (2 sticks) butter

5 pounds tomatoes, peeled, seeded, and chopped

3 cans condensed beef broth

8 cans condensed chicken broth

3 tablespoons balsamic vinegar

1 tablespoon sugar

1/3 cup dry white wine

Salt and pepper to taste

1/4 cup cornstarch, mixed with

1/2 cup water

GARNISH:

1 cup chopped fresh basil leaves

Crème fraîche (page 116)

Cook the leeks in butter until softened, not letting them brown. Add tomatoes, broth, vinegar, sugar, wine, salt, and pepper. Bring to a boil and simmer, partially covered, for 20 minutes.

Cool the soup slightly and puree it in the blender 2 cups at a time.

Pour soup back into saucepan, then add cornstarch mixture. Blend well, bring to a boil, and cook for 2 minutes. Garnish with fresh basil leaves and crème fraîche.

O NE of the great classic soups, this is elegant and yet easy to prepare. The soup may be made a day ahead, but the cream should not be added until the soup is reheated at serving time.

POTAGE CRESSONNIÈRE

SERVES: 4 TO 6

2 tablespoons butter

2 leeks, cleaned and chopped, minus the tough green leaves

3 medium-size potatoes, peeled and sliced

2 cans condensed chicken broth diluted with 2 cans water (or 5 cups homemade chicken stock)

1 bunch watercress

Salt and pepper to taste

1 cup heavy cream

Watercress leaves for garnish

Heat the butter in a large saucepan without letting it brown, then add the leeks and sauté them for a few minutes without browning. Add potatoes and chicken broth and water or chicken stock. Bring to a boil and simmer for 20 minutes. Add watercress (reserve a few leaves for garnish), salt, and pepper and turn off the heat immediately (otherwise the watercress will overcook and the soup will lose its lovely green color). Combine well.

Let soup cool slightly and puree in a blender 2 cups at a time. Add the cream.

Reheat the soup gently before serving or refrigerate and serve cold. Garnish with watercress leaves.

Among the spring and summer vegetables are (clockwise from top) asparagus, summer squash, purple and white eggplant, zucchini (the small ones with their edible blossoms still attached), and pattypan squash

Tomato Soup with Basil (page 32)

OPPOSITE: Chicken Noodle Soup (page 36)

CHICKEN NOODLE SOUP

SERVES: 6 TO 8

WHETHER or not you have a cold, to me this soup offers everything you need in the winter—warmth, comfort, and nurturing. It is my daughter's favorite soup, and I made it whenever she was home from college. Beatrice still loves to make a meal out of it.

The only time I make homemade chicken stock is for this soup; any other time I feel it is wasted. I also cook the chicken in the homemade stock to make it extra rich.

8 cups chicken stock (page 113)
1 roasting chicken (6 pounds)
3 carrots, chopped
2 celery stalks, chopped
1 red pepper, cut into cubes
1 bunch broccoli, cut into pieces
2 zucchini, cut into cubes
1/2 pound thin soup noodles, cooked in water according to package directions
1 bunch scallions, thinly sliced
Salt and pepper to taste
2 tablespoons chopped fresh parsley for garnish

Put the chicken stock into a large pot and bring to a boil, then add the chicken. When the stock comes to a boil again, lower the heat and simmer the chicken, covered, for about 1 hour.

Remove the chicken and let it cool. When it is cool enough to handle, remove the skin and bones. Discard them and cut the meat into chunks.

Skim as much fat from the broth as possible, then add the carrots, celery, and red pepper. Continue simmering for 10 minutes. Then add the broccoli and simmer for 5 minutes. Add the zucchini and simmer for 2 minutes. At the last minute add the cooked noodles, the scallions, salt, and pepper. Reheat, sprinkle with parsley, and serve.

HOT AND SOUR SOUP

SERVES: 6

THIS is a soup I learned to make from my friend Dee Wang. It is well worthwhile to look for the Chinese ingredients, which today are stocked in most good supermarkets.

The soup may be made ahead of time, but the scallions and eggs should not go in until it is reheated at serving time.

6 dried shiitaki mushrooms
1/3 cup dried cloud mushrooms
1/4 cup dried tiger lily flowers
2 quarts water
1 pound lean boneless pork, finely chopped
5 tablespoons white vinegar
2 tablespoons soy sauce
2 teaspoons salt
1/2 teaspoon pepper

1 teaspoon cayenne oil (see below)

2 cakes of soybean curd (tofu), chopped into small cubes

1 tablespoon cornstarch, mixed with ¼ cup water

1 tablespoon Oriental sesame oil

3 scallions, finely chopped

2 eggs, lightly beaten

Soak dried mushrooms and tiger lilies in warm water to cover for about half an hour.

Put the 2 quarts water and pork in a saucepan and bring to a boil. Simmer slowly for 10 minutes, skimming the surface every so often.

Cut the soaked shiitaki mushrooms in strips, removing and discarding the stems. If the cloud mushrooms are too large, cut them up a little.

Add the mushrooms and tiger lilies to the saucepan. Add the vinegar, soy sauce, salt, pepper, cayenne oil, and cubes of bean curd and bring to a boil, simmering for another 5 minutes. Add the cornstarch, sesame oil, and scallions. Bring to a boil again, mix in the eggs, and serve.

CAYENNE OIL:

½ cup vegetable oil

2 teaspoons cayenne

Pour oil into a small saucepan. Add cayenne. Heat slowly until the cayenne turns slightly brown. Turn off the heat and pour into a container, straining out the sediment. Leftover oil can be stored in the refrigerator.

HOT AND SOUR SOUP II

SERVES: 4

THIS is a quicker, easier version of this Chinese favorite, for when you have the urge but don't want to go through all that work.

1 can condensed chicken broth plus

1 can water

4 tablespoons white vinegar

2 tablespoons soy sauce

1 tablespoon sugar

¼ teaspoon cayenne

3 tablespoons cornstarch, mixed with a little water

1 bunch scallions, washed and finely chopped

1 cake of soybean curd (tofu), finely chopped

1 tablespoon Oriental sesame oil

2 eggs, mixed well with 1 tablespoon water

Combine the chicken broth, water, vinegar, soy sauce, sugar, and cayenne in a 3-quart saucepan and bring to a boil. Simmer for 2 minutes, then add the cornstarch.

Stir well and bring to a boil. Add the scallions, bean curd, sesame oil, and the eggs. Bring to a boil, stirring constantly, and serve.

CREAM OF WILD MUSHROOMS SOUP

SERVES: 6

Many markets carry one or more of these wild mushrooms (clockwise from upper right): *shiitake, chanterelle, cremini, morel, and oyster. In the center is the familiar cultivated champignon*

THIS soup combines fresh and dried wild mushrooms, for a delicate but woodsy flavor; I love the flavor of any mushroom.

1 ounce dried cèpes or porcini mushrooms
8 dried morels
2 cups warm water
4 tablespoons butter
3 shallots, chopped
1 teaspoon thyme
½ pound shiitake mushrooms, stems removed and brushed lightly
3 tablespoons flour
½ pound fresh chanterelles (or 1 1-pound can of chanterelles)
4 cans condensed chicken broth plus
2 cans water
Salt and pepper to taste
1 cup heavy cream
1 bunch fresh chives, chopped (or 2 tablespoons chopped fresh parsley), for garnish

Soak dried mushrooms together in 2 cups warm water for about 30 minutes.

Drain mushrooms through a fine strainer lined with cheesecloth (to eliminate sand). Reserve liquid.

Melt butter in a saucepan. Add shallots and thyme and sauté over medium heat until lightly browned. Add shiitake mushrooms and sauté for a few minutes. Sprinkle flour over mushrooms and combine well. Add chanterelles and drained dried mushrooms.

Add chicken broth, water, and reserved soaking liquid. Simmer for 30 minutes. Add salt and pepper to taste.

Puree soup briefly in a blender, 2 cups at a time, making sure that some sizable pieces of mushroom remain. Return to saucepan.

At serving time, add 1 cup heavy cream, combine well, and let soup come to a boil. Garnish with chopped chives or parsley.

COUNTRY VEGETABLE SOUP

SERVES: 6 TO 8

SINCE I love all vegetables, I vary the ingredients of this soup according to what looks good in the market. As far as I am concerned, the more, the merrier. Also, I sometimes add cooked dried white beans or chick peas the last 10 minutes of cooking time, which, along with a slice of my favorite whole-grain bread, makes it a complete meal.

2 tablespoons vegetable oil
2 entire leeks, cleaned and coarsely chopped
4 cans condensed chicken broth plus
4 cans water
4 carrots, coarsely chopped
4 stalks celery, coarsely chopped
2 red peppers, coarsely chopped

¹/₂ head white cabbage, sliced
¹/₂ pound green beans, ends removed and cut into 1-inch pieces
1 head broccoli, cleaned and cut into pieces
3 zucchini, cleaned and coarsely chopped
Salt and pepper to taste
4 tablespoons chopped fresh parsley

In a large saucepan, heat the vegetable oil and sauté the leeks for a few minutes until they are wilted but not brown.

Add the chicken broth, water, carrots, celery, peppers, and cabbage. Bring to a boil and simmer for 10 minutes. Add the green beans, broccoli, and zucchini and continue simmering for another 5 minutes. Season with salt and pepper to taste and add the parsley.

Broccoli, carrots, and beets are hardy and colorful winter vegetables

CREAM OF WHITE ASPARAGUS SOUP

SERVES: 4

UNTIL I came to America, I never saw a green asparagus. White asparagus is much more popular in Germany. There, all the ends and peels of the white asparagus were used to make a broth that was strained and used as the base for cream of asparagus soup. To this, the asparagus tips were added.

In America, I make this soup with canned white asparagus—the only time I ever use a canned vegetable—since it will be pureed. I find that the best canned asparagus is from Taiwan or the Far East; the French variety is too woody and too expensive.

To get rid of the asparagus fibers, stir vigorously with a whisk. The fibers will stick to the whisk when you lift it out of the soup. Shake off the whisk. Repeat this process several times for a smoother soup.

You may keep the ingredients for this soup on hand in your pantry and make it on the spur of the moment in 5 minutes. It can also be made several hours ahead.

1 10½-ounce can white asparagus
2 tablespoons butter
2 tablespoons flour
1 can condensed chicken broth plus
1 can water
½ cup heavy cream
Salt and pepper to taste
Finely chopped fresh parsley for garnish

Put the asparagus and the water in which it is packed into a blender and blend for 2 minutes.

In a heavy 3-quart saucepan, melt the butter, add the flour, and mix well. Cook for two minutes. Add the chicken broth, water, and pureed asparagus. Stir with a whisk until it boils (to avoid lumps). Simmer for 5 minutes.

Add the cream and season with salt and pepper to taste. Garnish with parsley.

GREEN ASPARAGUS SOUP

SERVES: 6

THE only time I eat asparagus is when it is in season in my area, and then I eat as much as I can. I make this soup the day after serving the asparagus tips as a vegetable when I have all the ends left. I also keep asparagus stock in the freezer. I usually have quite a bit, as I don't like to throw out the asparagus ends, and I find it easy to make them into stock.

NOTE: You may enrich this soup further by adding 2 egg yolks, mixed with ¼ cup of the heavy cream, just before serving. Make sure that the soup does not come to a boil again, or the egg yolks will curdle.

STOCK:
4 cups asparagus ends and peels
5 cups chicken broth
Salt and pepper to taste

SOUP:

> *3 tablespoons butter*
> *3 tablespoons flour*
> *5 cups asparagus stock*
> *1 cup asparagus cut in 1-inch pieces*
> *1 cup heavy cream*

YIELD: 5 CUPS

To make the stock: Combine the asparagus ends and peels with the chicken broth in a large saucepan. Season with salt and pepper, bring to a boil, and simmer for 30 minutes.

Put the stock through a strainer, pressing down on the asparagus in order to extract all the juices. Discard the asparagus.

To make the soup: In a large, heavy saucepan, melt the butter. Add the flour, stirring and cooking this roux for about 3 minutes without letting it brown.

Add the asparagus stock and asparagus, bring to a boil, and simmer for 6 minutes. Add the heavy cream (see NOTE). Taste and adjust seasoning. Bring to a boil and serve.

BLACK BEAN SOUP

SERVES: 8

T HERE are as many versions of this soup as there are people who make it. This is my favorite recipe. I often serve it as a main luncheon course, along with a light salad and dessert.

> *4 thick slices bacon, chopped*
> *3 stalks celery, chopped*
> *3 onions, chopped*
> *1 pound black beans, soaked overnight and drained*
> *1 ham bone*
> *2 bay leaves*
> *2 cloves garlic, put through a garlic press*
> *1/2 teaspoon cayenne pepper*
> *2 cans condensed beef broth plus*
> *6 cans water*
> *Salt and pepper to taste*
> *8 lemon slices for garnish*

In a heavy 4-quart saucepan, sauté the bacon pieces until lightly browned. Add the celery and onions and sauté for 3 minutes without letting them brown. Add the rest of the ingredients. Combine well and bring to a boil. Simmer on a low flame for about 2½ hours, stirring every so often.

Remove what meat there is on the bone, put the meat in the soup, and discard the bone. Cool the soup slightly and put through a blender 2 cups at a time. Reheat and serve with thin slices of lemon on top.

RUSSIAN BORSCHT

SERVES: 8

I don't know if this is a genuine Russian borscht, but I do know that it tastes good to me, so I don't worry about its authenticity.

This makes a great meal when served with black bread. If you prefer a vegetable borscht, simply eliminate the beef.

NOTE: Fresh beets give this soup a better color, but canned may also be used.

1 1/2 pounds lean beef (top round or eye round)
3 cans condensed beef broth diluted with 5 cans water (or 8 cups water)
3 entire leeks, cleaned and coarsely chopped
2 stalks celery, chopped
3 carrots, coarsely chopped
3 sprigs parsley
1 bay leaf
2 cloves garlic, put through a garlic press
Salt and pepper to taste
1/2 head white cabbage, coarsely chopped
3 medium potatoes, coarsely chopped
2 medium onions, sliced
1 pound fresh beets, cooked, peeled, and diced, or canned beets, diced
1 cup sour cream

Dice the beef and put it into a saucepan with the beef broth and water. Bring slowly to a boil and skim carefully as the scum from the beef rises to the surface.

Add the leeks, celery, carrots, parsley, bay leaf, garlic; salt, and pepper. Bring to a boil and simmer, covered, for one hour, skimming from time to time. Add the cabbage, potatoes, and onions. Bring to a boil and continue simmering for another 30 minutes.

Finally, add the beets and simmer for another 5 minutes. Be sure to remove the bay leaf before serving.

Put a spoonful of sour cream on each serving and serve hot.

CAULIFLOWER AND STILTON CHEESE SOUP

SERVES: 8

THIS elegant and easy soup is another recipe from my tenure as executive chef of *Gourmet* magazine's dining room.

The distinctive Stilton cheese flavor is subtle, yet it masks the cauliflower taste some people dislike.

1 large onion, chopped
1 tablespoon minced garlic
3 tablespoons butter
3 tablespoons flour
2 cups condensed chicken broth
2 cups water
1 large head cauliflower, separated into flowerets

1 cup milk
¹⁄₃ cup Stilton, crumbled
2 tablespoons lemon juice, or to taste

GARNISH:
Crumbled Stilton
Chopped fresh parsley

In a large pot, sauté onion and garlic in 3 tablespoons butter over medium heat until golden. Add 3 tablespoons flour and stir for 3 minutes without browning. Add chicken broth and water. Stir constantly until it boils. Add cauliflower and simmer, covered, until cauliflower is tender, about 10 to 15 minutes.

Cool soup slightly, then puree it in a blender 2 cups at a time.

At serving time, add milk and heat soup. Add Stilton cheese, stirring just until cheese melts. Add lemon juice, taste, and adjust seasonings.

Serve garnished with crumbled Stilton and parsley.

MINTED CANTALOUPE AND HONEYDEW SOUP

SERVES: 6

I am not a big fan of cold soups, unless they are fruit soups and, like this one, look beautiful as well as taste great. This is also very easy to make.

If you enjoy this soup, I suggest that when cantaloupe and honeydew are in season, you buy a batch, seed them, cut them in chunks, and put them in the freezer. After a quick partial thaw, they will be ready to be whipped up into this soup in no time.

It seems to me that this soup lends itself perfectly to the poolside.

CANTALOUPE SOUP:
> $2^1/_2$ cups cantaloupe, seeded, rind cut off, and chopped
> $1^1/_2$ teaspoons chopped fresh mint
> $1^1/_2$ tablespoons superfine sugar
> $^1/_4$ cup dry white wine

HONEYDEW SOUP:
> $2^1/_2$ cups honeydew, seeded, rind cut off, and chopped
> $1^1/_2$ teaspoons chopped fresh mint
> $1^1/_2$ tablespoons superfine sugar
> $^1/_4$ cup dry white wine

GARNISH:
> Plain yogurt
> Mint sprigs

To make the cantaloupe soup: In a blender, puree the cantaloupe, mint, sugar, and wine until the sugar is dissolved. Transfer the puree to a glass pitcher or bowl. Refrigerate until well chilled.

To make the honeydew soup: Repeat this process with the honeydew.

To serve: Simultaneously pour some of each soup into individual bowls so that one soup is on the left half of the bowl and the other is on the right half. Put a dollop of yogurt on the soup and rest a mint sprig on top of the yogurt.

SALADS

ONE of the great things about salads is that they are so versatile—they can be served as a first course, a main course, a separate course following the entrée, or even dessert. I love salads, and in the summer, when so many wonderful fresh ingredients are available, I eat one for lunch almost every day.

In my dining room, I always serve a green salad after the main course at dinner. For lunch I serve more substantial mixtures of vegetables with meat or whole grains along with the greens.

A good salad requires:

1) fresh ingredients;
3) thoroughly washed greens;
3) a good dressing.

In my dining room, Heidi is in charge of (among many other things) washing the greens. She recommends removing all yellow or wilted leaves and then putting the greens in cold water and swishing them around until the dirt settles. Then she removes the greens and rinses them again in cold water. Greens like arugula or spinach, which are grown in sandy soil, need particular attention. For those, she fills the sink once more with cold water and lets them soak for a few minutes. Then she drains them and spins them dry in a salad spinner.

Heidi then wraps the greens in dry paper towels, seals them in a plastic bag, labels the bag, and refrigerates it until ready for use. If you clean your greens and prepare your dressing in the morning, all you will have to do at dinnertime is toss it together.

Presentation is always important. With all the varied textures and colors of salad ingredients, the salad can easily be made visually appealing as well as pleasing to the taste. Chilling the plates and forks you use is a very nice touch. (I put my salad forks in the freezer two hours prior to serving.)

GREEN SALAD WITH STILTON CHEESE

SERVES: 6 TO 8

THIS is the salad I generally serve in my dining room, especially in the winter, when Stilton cheese is the perfect complement to these greens. Maggi Seasoning, which I use in almost all my salad dressings, is to Germans what soy sauce is to the Japanese. It is an extract of various vegetables. You can buy it in most supermarkets.

To toast hazelnuts, put the chopped nuts on a cookie sheet and bake for approximately 10 minutes in a 350° F. oven or until they turn golden. Check occasionally to make sure they do not get too dark.

1 bunch watercress, washed, dried, and large stems removed
1 bunch arugula, washed and dried
1 bunch red-leaf lettuce, washed, dried, and cut or torn into bite-size pieces
2 Belgian endives, julienned
¼ pound Stilton cheese, crumbled
¼ cup hazelnuts, chopped and toasted

DRESSING:
½ cup vegetable oil
2 tablespoons hazelnut oil
2 tablespoons cider vinegar
1 teaspoon honey
1 teaspoon Maggi Seasoning

Toss all salad greens together. Combine dressing ingredients in a blender and mix well, or combine in a large bowl and whisk together until blended.

Just before serving, toss salad with dressing. Put portions on individual chilled plates and sprinkle with hazelnuts and Stilton cheese.

BULGUR SALAD

SERVES: 6

I often have this salad for dinner when I am alone.

Since it contains no greens, this salad may be made several hours ahead.

NOTE: Couscous may be substituted for the bulgur, and it is even easier to prepare than the cracked wheat. If your package of couscous does not have directions, bring 1½ cups chicken broth or water to a boil and pour it over 1 cup couscous. Cover and let sit for 5 minutes, then fluff it with a fork.

2 cups water or chicken broth
1 cup bulgur (cracked wheat)
1 cucumber
2 tomatoes, cut into small cubes
1 red bell pepper, washed, seeded, and finely chopped
1 green bell pepper, washed, seeded, and finely chopped
1 bunch scallions, thinly sliced

Bulgur Salad

Salads have become more interesting since farmers have begun to cultivate a variety of greens, such as (clockwise from upper right) oakleaf lettuce, red Boston, dandelion, watercress, arugula, frisé, lollo rosso, bibb, and red oakleaf lettuce. Belgian endive and radicchio (center) contribute distinctive flavors and colors

Fresh basil is the perfect complement to ripe tomatoes

Tomatoes with Basil (page 48)

½ cup finely chopped fresh parsley
Salt and pepper to taste
4 tablespoons lemon juice
¼ cup olive oil

Bring the water or chicken broth to a boil in a small saucepan. Slowly add the bulgur. Cover the pan and simmer over low heat for 15 minutes, or until all of the water has been absorbed. Transfer the bulgur to a bowl and let cool to room temperature.

In the meantime, peel the cucumber and cut in half lengthwise. Remove the seeds with a spoon, sprinkle with salt, and let sit for 10 minutes. Drain the cucumber. Cut it into small cubes and add with the remaining ingredients to the cooled bulgur. Combine well and serve.

TOMATOES WITH BASIL

SERVES: 6

THE only time I have this salad is when the New Jersey Beefsteak tomatoes are in season. They are truly one of the great gifts of God and the farmer. I overindulge in these tomatoes when they are available because the season is so short.

This may be served as a salad course or as a first course. When serving as a first course, I like to combine it with slices of fresh mozzarella cheese.

6 ripe tomatoes
3 tablespoons virgin olive oil
2 tablespoons balsamic or cider vinegar
2 tablespoons finely chopped Bermuda onion
4 tablespoons finely chopped fresh basil
Salt and pepper to taste

Wash tomatoes and remove the brown stem end. Cut them into ¼-inch slices and arrange, overlapping, on a serving platter. Drizzle the olive oil over them and sprinkle with the vinegar, then the onions, basil, salt, and pepper.

Let stand and marinate for at least 15 minutes before serving.

CHINESE CHICKEN SALAD

SERVES: 4

NOTE: For a spicy, Szechuan taste, substitute hot sesame oil for the Oriental sesame oil.

½ pound bean sprouts
1 roasted red pepper (see directions on page 114), julienned (or 1 3-ounce jar pimientos, cut into thin strips)
1 head romaine lettuce, cut into thin strips
½ head iceberg lettuce, cut into thin strips
4 chicken breasts, poached, cooled, and cut into strips
1 seedless cucumber, cut into thin slices
¼ pound snow peas, steamed and cut in half lengthwise
1 tablespoon sesame seeds, toasted
1 tablespoon coarsely chopped fresh coriander (2 stalks)

DRESSING:
½ cup vegetable oil
1 tablespoon Oriental sesame oil
2 tablespoons cider vinegar or rice wine vinegar
1 tablespoon soy sauce
1 teaspoon honey

Put all dressing ingredients in a blender and blend until well combined.

Put bean sprouts, red pepper, romaine, and iceberg lettuce in a bowl and pour most of the dressing over. Arrange on a serving platter or on individual plates. Place chicken, cucumber slices, and snow peas on top. Sprinkle with sesame seeds and coriander. Drizzle a bit of extra dressing on chicken.

ALTHOUGH I am not a big fan of mayonnaise salads, I happen to like this one, since the flavor of the curry cuts the mayonnaise taste. The curry is a subtle taste, but the addition of the chutney gives the salad more zip. Although I use homemade mayonnaise for this salad, no one will notice it if a good commercial mayonnaise, such as Hellmann's, is substituted.

This salad is great as a summer luncheon platter or tucked into a pita. It is also wonderful combined with fresh pineapple and served in a pineapple shell. I envision this salad served at poolside or in a summer garden.

NOTE: The salad can be made up to a day ahead and kept refrigerated, but it should be taken out of the refrigerator about half an hour before serving. When served too cold, it loses some of its flavor.

4 cups boneless cooked chicken, about 2 whole breasts, cut into bite-size pieces
2 Granny Smith apples, peeled, cored, cut into quarters, and sliced crosswise
1 cup pecans, broken in quarters or coarsely chopped
1 cup pineapple chunks in their own juice, drained

DRESSING:
¹/₂ cup mayonnaise
¹/₄ cup vegetable oil
1 tablespoon curry powder
1 tablespoon chutney
2 tablespoons cider vinegar

GARNISH:
Romaine lettuce
Chopped fresh parsley
Tomato roses

Put all dressing ingredients in a blender and blend until well combined.

Put the salad ingredients in a bowl, pour the dressing over, and mix well. Refrigerate for at least 30 minutes.

To serve, mound the salad on romaine leaves and garnish with parsley and tomato roses.

CURRIED CHICKEN SALAD

SERVES: 4

Breast of Duck Salad with Spiced Bene-dictine Dressing (page 52)

With its variety of greens and sprinkling of edible flowers, mesclun makes a pretty and delectable salad

OPPOSITE: *Chinese Chicken Salad (page 48)*

51

BREAST OF DUCK SALAD WITH SPICED BENEDICTINE DRESSING

SERVES: 4

WHILE doing lunches for *Gourmet* magazine, occasionally I would be asked to create a dish using a particular ingredient. In this case, I was asked to create a recipe using Benedictine, a wonderful liqueur that adds a unique fire to a recipe. I think you will enjoy this unusual salad, which may be served either as a luncheon salad or a first course.

You can cook the duck breasts and make the dressing several hours ahead of time, but remember to warm the dressing before assembling the salad.

NOTE: Leftover leg of lamb may be used instead of duck breast.

2 whole duck breasts, cut in half and trimmed
4 tablespoons vegetable oil
2 tablespoons minced shallots
2 teaspoons minced garlic
1 carrot, finely chopped
½ cup Benedictine
¼ cup freshly squeezed orange juice
¼ cup balsamic vinegar
½ cup brown stock (or ½ cup condensed beef broth)
3 whole cloves
2 tablespoons minced fresh thyme
Nutmeg, grated, to taste
½ cup extra virgin olive oil
1 endive, julienned
1 small radicchio, julienned
2 bunches arugula, washed and trimmed

Rub duck breasts with salt and pepper. Heat 4 tablespoons oil in a large skillet over moderately high heat. Add the duck breasts, skin side down. Sauté until golden, turn, and reduce heat. Cook until pink inside, about 5 minutes. Remove the duck to a plate and set aside.

Pour off all but 2 tablespoons fat from the skillet. Over moderate heat, sauté the shallots, garlic, and carrot for 2 minutes. Deglaze the skillet with the Benedictine. Add the orange juice, balsamic vinegar, and the brown stock. Bring to a boil. Add the cloves, thyme, and nutmeg. Lower heat and simmer until reduced to about 1 cup of liquid.

Strain the dressing and whisk in the olive oil.

To serve, cut duck breasts in ½-inch slivers. Combine salad greens and arrange them on individual plates. Put the duck over the salad and pour warm Benedictine dressing over all. Serve while still slightly warm.

THERE is nothing in the world as satisfying as a good potato salad. In Germany there are probably as many German potato salads as there are German families. Everyone has his own favorite version, and this is mine.

Whether you slice the potatoes or cut them into chunks, peel them or don't peel them, the secret of the good flavor is to pour the dressing over the potatoes while they are still warm. They will not absorb the dressing once they are cold.

The long, seedless cucumbers or small cukes give the best flavor. The regular cucumbers are heavily waxed, so they must be peeled and their seeds, which are completely indigestible, removed. I peel the long, seedless variety as well. If you do not want to have onion in the potato salad, add the onion to the dressing ingredients before blending. You may also add a bit of chopped dill pickle if you like.

The salad may be made several hours ahead, but it should not be refrigerated. Simply cover and leave at room temperature.

3 pounds small potatoes
1 large seedless cucumber or 3 small cukes
½ Bermuda or red onion, finely chopped
1 dill pickle, chopped, optional

DRESSING:
¾ cup vegetable oil
2 tablespoons Dijon or Pommery mustard
4 tablespoons cider vinegar
4 stalks fresh parsley
4 stalks fresh dill
Salt and pepper to taste

Steam the potatoes in their skins until a sharp knife pierces them easily but before they get soft. (They will continue to cook in the skin for a while after you remove them.)

While potatoes are cooling, peel and thinly slice the cucumbers and chop the onion and, if using, the pickle.

When the potatoes are cool enough to handle, peel if desired and slice or chop them. Combine with the cucumber, onion, and pickle.

Put dressing ingredients in a blender and blend thoroughly. While potatoes are still warm, pour dressing over salad and toss well. Cover and store at room temperature. Before serving, taste and add more vinegar if necessary.

POTATO AND CUCUMBER SALAD

SERVES: 4 TO 6

IN the winter, my lunch usually consists of a great soup. In the summer, I usually have a wonderful salad. This is one of my favorites. I created it for *Gourmet* magazine when I was executive chef of their dining room. It is a wonderful first-course salad as well.

A mixture of wild young greens and edible flowers, called mesclun, is now available in some stores. If it is unobtainable, use a combination of arugula, washed and dried; watercress, washed, dried, and stems removed; endive, julienned; red-leaf lettuce, washed, dried, and torn in pieces; and radicchio, sliced.

Now that wild mushrooms are commonly available, I make this salad often, particularly when I want to have a meatless meal. If you cannot find shiitake mushrooms, chanterelles, cèpes, or other wild mushrooms, use regular cultivated mushrooms that are very fresh.

The peppers may be roasted (see directions on page 114) and cut ahead of time, but everything else should be done just before serving.

½ pound fresh mushrooms, wild or cultivated
2 tablespoons vegetable oil
8 cups assorted greens, approximately (see above)
1 roasted red pepper, cut into strips
1 roasted yellow pepper, cut into strips
1 tablespoon each assorted fresh herbs, such as chervil, parsley, chives

BALSAMIC DRESSING:
½ cup vegetable oil
1 tablespoon hazelnut oil
2 tablespoons balsamic vinegar
1 teaspoon honey

Sauté mushrooms in 2 tablespoons vegetable oil until soft.

Combine dressing ingredients in a blender and blend well.

Toss greens with most of the dressing. Put on a chilled plate. Scatter mushrooms and red and yellow pepper strips over greens. Drizzle additional dressing over. Sprinkle with fresh herbs.

MUSHROOM AND WILD GREENS SALAD

SERVES: 4 TO 6

WALTER'S CHICKEN SALAD

SERVES: 4 TO 6

THIS is what I have been serving these days when I have someone over for lunch. With a light soup and dessert, it makes an impressive meal.

To ingredients of Mushroom and Wild Greens Salad (page 55), add:
> *2 chicken breasts, cut in half*
> *1 teaspoon Spike Vegetable Seasoning*
> *3 tablespoons lemon juice*
> *4 tablespoons vegetable oil*
> *½ cucumber (or 2 small cukes), peeled and sliced*
> *12 stalks asparagus, steamed*

Season chicken breasts with Spike Seasoning and lemon juice. Sauté in 4 tablespoons vegetable oil for 3 minutes on each side. Cut chicken into strips.

Arrange Mushroom and Wild Greens Salad on plates, adding the sliced cucumber. Place warm strips of chicken and asparagus stalks on top of salad. Drizzle with balsamic dressing (page 55).

SALADE NIÇOISE

SERVES: 4

THIS is one of the all-time great classic summer salads. It combines the best and freshest tastes of summertime. Since it is rarely made well in restaurants, it is always good to make at home.

> *3 tomatoes, washed and quartered*
> *6 radishes, washed, with tops removed*
> *2 heads Bibb lettuce, leaves separated and washed*
> *1 7-ounce can solid white tuna, drained*
> *8 anchovy fillets*
> *2 hard-boiled eggs, quartered*
> *8 ripe olives, preferably Niçoise*
> *½ Bermuda onion, thinly sliced*
> *¼ pound French haricots verts or regular green beans, steamed*
> *4 small potatoes, steamed and quartered*
> *1 tablespoon finely chopped fresh parsley for garnish*

DRESSING:
> *½ cup vegetable oil*
> *2 tablespoons cider vinegar*
> *1 tablespoon Pommery mustard*
> *1 teaspoon honey*

Arrange salad ingredients attractively on a decorative platter or in a salad bowl.

Combine dressing ingredients in a blender or whisk together in a large bowl.

Drizzle salad with dressing and top with chopped fresh parsley.

MAIN COURSES

A tournedo is simply a thick steak cut from the fillet, a good choice when serving only a few guests. This recipe has been one of my favorite standbys for many years, as it can be done very quickly. However, it cannot be made ahead of time.

The sauce also works well with shell steak or any other kind of steak, as long as the meat is always browned first, because the glaze from the browning gives the sauce its savor.

NOTE: The only green peppercorns worth buying are those freeze-dried or packed in brine. The vinegar-packed ones are rather rubbery and have an inferior taste.

6 tournedos of beef
Salt and pepper to taste
2 tablespoons butter
1 tablespoon vegetable oil
4 shallots, finely chopped
¾ cup condensed beef broth
½ cup dry red wine
1 teaspoon meat extract (Bovril)
2 tablespoons green peppercorns (see above)
1 teaspoon cornstarch mixed with a little water

Season the tournedos with salt and pepper. Heat the butter and oil in a heavy sauté pan and add the tournedos. Brown them well on each side. Remove them from the pan and put aside.

Add the shallots to the pan and sauté them for about 3 minutes. Add the beef broth, wine, meat extract, and peppercorns. Simmer over low heat for about 10 minutes.

Return the tournedos to this sauce and simmer to desired tenderness. (The meat should feel springy to the touch when pressed with a finger.) Remove the meat to a plate.

Thicken the sauce with the cornstarch mixture and pour over the meat.

TOURNEDOS MADAGASCAR

SERVES: 6

Osso Bucco (page 62)

Marinated Leg of Lamb (page 62), with Couscous (page 85) and Caponata (page 81)

Veal Marengo (page 61)

59

VITELLO TONNATO

SERVES: 4 TO 6

FOR a summer buffet, you can't beat this dish. It looks great, tastes wonderful, and can be made the day before serving.

2-pound boned leg of veal, rolled and secured with string
3 tablespoons lemon juice
4 cups water
1 cup white wine
1 onion
3 cloves
1 bay leaf
2 stalks celery with leaves, cut into 1-inch pieces
2 carrots, cut into 1-inch pieces
6 sprigs parsley
1 tablespoon salt
6 peppercorns
1 cup tuna fish
4 anchovy fillets
¼ cup olive oil
¾ cup vegetable oil
6 tablespoons lemon juice
¼ cup drained capers

GARNISH:
Several sprigs of parsley
Lemon roses

Rub the veal with the lemon juice and set aside.

Combine the water, wine, onion, cloves, bay leaf, celery, carrots, parsley, salt, and peppercorns in a large kettle and bring slowly to a boil. Add the veal, making sure it is completely covered by the liquid, and again bring to a boil. Cover the pan and simmer for about 1½ hours. Remove the meat from the broth and cool it thoroughly.

In a blender or food processor combine the tuna, anchovies, olive oil, vegetable oil, lemon juice, and capers. Blend until smooth.

After the meat has cooled, slice it thin and arrange it on a platter. Garnish with fresh parsley and lemon roses and serve with sauce on the side.

VEAL MARENGO

SERVES: 6

THIS recipe was supposedly created with chicken by Napoleon's chef at the Battle of Waterloo. Napoleon may have lost the battle, but he certainly ate well that day.

This is a good dish for a crowd, because it can be prepared the day before. Just add the tomato on the day you are serving it.

2 tablespoons vegetable oil
2 tablespoons olive oil
2 pounds shoulder of veal, cut into 1-inch pieces
Salt and pepper
2 tablespoons flour
2 tablespoons tomato paste
1 clove garlic, put through a garlic press
1 cup dry white wine
1 can condensed chicken broth
1 bouquet garni: 3 sprigs parsley, 1 bay leaf, 1 celery leaf, tied together with cotton string
1 teaspoon thyme
2 tablespoons butter
20 small white onions
1 tablespoon sugar
½ pound mushrooms, whole if small, quartered if large
1 tomato, peeled, seeded, and cut into eighths
1 tablespoon chopped fresh parsley for garnish

In a large, heavy casserole or sauté pan, heat the oils and add just enough veal pieces so that they do not touch one another. Brown them well on all sides. Remove them from pan with a slotted spoon and continue until all the remaining veal is browned.

Return veal to pan. Sprinkle it with salt, pepper, and the flour. Stir and sauté for a few minutes, then add the tomato paste, garlic, wine, chicken broth, bouquet garni, and thyme. Bring to a boil and simmer for 1 hour.

In the meantime, melt the butter in a heavy sauté pan. Add the onions, sprinkle them with the sugar, and sauté until they are nicely browned, then toss in the mushrooms, adding more butter if necessary, and brown them. Add the mushrooms and onions to the casserole after the stew has simmered for an hour. Continue simmering for 20 minutes. Add tomato and simmer for 10 more minutes. Remove the bouquet garni. Garnish with the parsley.

OSSO BUCCO

SERVES: 4

BESIDES being one of the great classic Italian dishes, this recipe is praiseworthy because it can be made well ahead of time—even the day before—and simply reheated at serving time. It is also wonderful for entertaining a larger group, since the recipe can be easily doubled or tripled. (However, do not add more bay leaf.)

Saffron Rissotto (page 85) or saffron rice, which you can get already seasoned in the supermarket, complements it beautifully, and an arugula salad will complete the meal.

If you happen to have marrow spoons, now is the time to use them: the marrow inside the bones is definitely a taste treat.

⅓ cup flour
1 teaspoon salt
¼ teaspoon pepper
4 veal shanks, cut into 2-inch pieces (ask the butcher to do this)
3 tablespoons olive oil
1 cup coarsely chopped onions
1 cup coarsely chopped carrots
1 cup coarsely chopped celery
2 cloves garlic, crushed
1 cup peeled and coarsely chopped tomatoes
1 cup white wine
1 teaspoon basil
1 teaspoon thyme
1 bay leaf
3 tablespoons chopped fresh parsley

Combine the flour, salt, and pepper. Turn the veal shanks in the mixture and shake off excess flour.

Heat the olive oil in a large, heavy pot. Sauté the veal shanks, turning them until all sides are nicely browned. Remove from pot and set aside.

Add onions, carrots, celery, and garlic to the pot and sauté for about 5 minutes. Add tomatoes, wine, basil, thyme, and bay leaf. Mix well and bring to a boil.

Put the veal shanks back into the pot and simmer, covered, for about 2 hours.

Just before serving, add the parsley.

MARINATED LEG OF LAMB

SERVES: 8

FRESH American lamb is the best kind to use; I find that New Zealand lamb has a slightly muttony flavor. I ask my butcher to bone and butterfly the leg of lamb for me. This simply means that he removes the bone and cuts the leg open. My butcher is always happy to give me the bones and the trimmings. From these, I make a stock and add the stock to the marinade to make more sauce.

When I get my lamb home, I retrim it to get all the fat off. I also cut the sinews from the bottom of the leg and add them to the stock. The leg of lamb may be trimmed and marinated the day before serving. Keep it well covered in the refrigerator.

This recipe calls for fresh lemon juice and fresh garlic. If you have fresh rosemary, great! If not, Spice Islands dried rosemary is a good choice. Rubbing the herb between the palms before adding releases the volatile oils. Kikkoman, I find, is the best soy sauce. For those on a low-salt diet, a low-sodium variety is available.

It is important not to overcook lamb. I treat it like a steak, cooking it to rosy rare and never letting it get well done.

This recipe is also fabulous done on a barbecue grill. Leftovers taste wonderful julienned in a salad.

1 leg of lamb, 6 to 7 pounds, boned and butterflied

MARINADE:
  Juice of 1 lemon
  2 cloves garlic, put through a garlic press
  2 teaspoons fresh rosemary (or 1 teaspoon dried)
  ¼ cup soy sauce

Remove all excess fat from the lamb. Rub both sides well with lemon juice, garlic, and rosemary. Sprinkle on the soy sauce and let the lamb marinate with these ingredients for at least 30 minutes or for several hours in the refrigerator.

Preheat the broiler for 5 minutes. Season the lamb with salt and pepper to taste (do not season earlier) and broil for about 15 minutes on each side. The cooking time varies according to the thickness of the lamb and the desired doneness, but it is best if removed when at least lightly pink inside.

LAMB CASSEROLE

SERVES: 6

NOW that stews are chic again, by all means try this on a cold fall or winter night. I served this even when it was not yet chic, because I consider it one of the all-time great dishes.

Sometimes I add some canned white beans or flageolets to make an even heartier dish. I generally serve the stew with some fresh bread and a light salad.

This casserole may be made the day before and even frozen ahead of time.

  3 tablespoons vegetable oil
  3 pounds lean lamb from the leg, cut into 1-inch pieces
  2 onions, chopped
  2 cloves garlic, put through a garlic press
  2 tablespoons summer savory
  1 teaspoon thyme
  1 tablespoon tomato paste
  1 32-ounce can tomatoes, undrained
  1 can condensed beef broth
  1 can water

Salt and pepper to taste
2 red peppers, coarsely chopped
2 green peppers, coarsely chopped
1 pound fresh green beans, ends removed, cut into 1-inch lengths
Chopped fresh parsley for garnish

Heat the oil in a large, heavy sauté pan, then add just enough lamb pieces so that they do not touch one another and brown them. Remove from pan with a slotted spoon and continue until all the remaining lamb is browned. Set aside.

Add the onions and garlic to the pan and sauté until lightly browned. Return the lamb to the pan and add the summer savory, thyme, tomato paste, tomatoes, beef broth, water, salt, and pepper. Bring to a boil and simmer, covered, for 1 hour. Add the peppers and green beans and simmer for another 30 minutes.

Serve with chopped fresh parsley on top.

IRISH LAMB STEW

SERVES: 8

WHEN I was Jacqueline Kennedy's chef, I used to make this on Saint Patrick's Day. However, it is fine most times of the year. It can be made a day ahead; in fact, the flavor improves when it is made ahead.

NOTE: Whenever you have small white onions to cook, drop them into boiling water for 1 minute, remove them and peel them, then cut a small cross into the root end of each onion to keep it from falling apart as it cooks.

4 pounds shoulder of lamb, trimmed of fat and cut into 2-inch squares
3 cups condensed beef broth
4 cups water
3 medium onions, coarsely chopped
4 potatoes, coarsely chopped
3 entire leeks, tough leaves removed, coarsely chopped
4 stalks celery, coarsely chopped
3 cloves garlic, minced
1 bay leaf
2 tablespoons summer savory
1 teaspoon salt
1 teaspoon freshly ground pepper
20 small white onions (see above)
4 medium potatoes, cut into eighths
6 carrots, cut into 1½-inch pieces
4 tablespoons finely chopped fresh parsley

Put the lamb into a large saucepan and add the beef broth, water, onions, potatoes, leeks, celery, garlic, bay leaf, summer savory, salt, and pepper. Bring to a boil and simmer over low heat for 1 hour, stirring occasionally.

Transfer the meat to a casserole or Dutch oven. Skim excess fat from the broth and allow it to cool slightly. Remove the bay leaf.

Put the broth and vegetables into a blender 2 cups at a time and puree the mixture. Pour this sauce over the lamb. Add the other vegetables to the casserole and simmer another 30 minutes. Add the parsley, combine well, and serve.

HAM WITH GLAZE AND MUSTARD SAUCE

SERVES: 16

T HIS recipe is great anytime you want to entertain without fuss. Basically, you prepare the ham for roasting, stick it in the oven, and simply baste occasionally. Since you are using a cured ham, it is more a process of heating through than cooking.

I find that Schaller and Weber hams are the best. They are now nationally distributed, so you should be able to find them or order them through your butcher. (Here is another way that it pays to be nice to your butcher. If you develop a good relationship with him or her, he will be more likely to go out of his way for you.) I buy the ham with the bone in and then make pea soup or lentil soup the next day with the bone. Leftover ham is great in a salad.

1 ham, 12 to 14 pounds
2 cups apple cider
1 teaspoon Colman's dry mustard
1/2 cup cider vinegar
2 cups dried apricots, soaked in
1 cup apple cider
3 apples, peeled, cored, and chopped
1 teaspoon rosemary, lightly crushed
Salt and pepper

Preheat oven to 325° F.

Place the ham, fat side up, in a large roasting pan, preferably on a rack. If using a meat thermometer, place it where it does not touch the bone.

After 1 hour of roasting, add the apple cider, mustard, vinegar, apricots with their soaking liquid, apples, and rosemary. Season the ham with salt and pepper.

Continue roasting the ham, basting it every 20 minutes for the remainder of the roasting time (approximately 25 minutes per pound). In the case of a 14-pound ham, roast close to 6 hours, or until the meat thermometer reaches 170° F.

THIS is another classic chicken dish that will remain with us for all time. I cooked this often when I was with Jacqueline Kennedy, and over twenty years later, it is just as good.

It can be made several hours ahead and reheated.

1 chicken, about 3 pounds, cut into eighths
Juice of 1 lemon
1 tablespoon thyme
3 tablespoons vegetable oil
Salt and pepper to taste
4 shallots, chopped
½ clove garlic, put through a garlic press
1 tablespoon thyme
2 tablespoons flour
1 can condensed chicken broth
1 cup white wine
⅓ cup pitted black and green olives
Chopped fresh parsley for garnish

Rub lemon juice and 1 tablespoon thyme into chicken. Let marinate for about 15 minutes.

In a heavy sauté pan, heat the vegetable oil. Season the chicken with salt and pepper and brown it on all sides. Remove the chicken and set aside.

Sauté the shallots and garlic in the same pan until lightly browned. Add 1 tablespoon thyme and the flour and combine well. Add the chicken broth and white wine and bring to a boil, stirring with a whisk.

Return the browned chicken to the pan and simmer on low heat for 20 minutes, then add the olives and cook an additional 10 minutes.

Serve garnished with chopped fresh parsley.

CHICKEN WITH THYME

SERVES: 4 TO 6

THIS was one of the dishes I taught when traveling around the country with my cooking school. Amazingly, we sometimes got one hundred taste samples out of one little chicken.

With this recipe I serve couscous (page 85), which goes particularly well with it. The chicken may be made several hours ahead and reheated.

NOTE: Flambéing the Calvados is an important part of this recipe, but doing it demands taking precautions. Since the fat from the meat will feed the flames, flambé only if you have high ceilings or a clean metal exhaust hood over your stove. Otherwise, you can remove the chicken from the pan, put it on a heatproof platter, and pour the ignited Calvados over it. I heat it in a large stainless steel soup ladle held directly over the hot burner and then light it. Make sure to stand back from the flames.

CHICKEN VINAIGRE

SERVES: 4 TO 6

Chicken with Thyme

1 chicken, about 3 pounds, cut into eighths
Salt and pepper to taste
3 tablespoons vegetable oil
2 tablespoons (1 ounce) Calvados (French apple brandy)
2 tablespoons finely chopped shallots
2 apples, preferably Granny Smith, peeled, cored, and sliced
1/2 cup dry white wine
1 can condensed chicken broth
1/2 cup cider vinegar
1 teaspoon honey
1 tablespoon Pommery mustard
Chopped fresh parsley for garnish

Season the chicken with salt and pepper. Heat the oil in a heavy sauté pan and sauté the chicken until brown on all sides. Heat the Calvados and pour it, flaming, over the chicken. (See NOTE.) When the flame burns out, remove the chicken from the sauté pan and set aside.

Add the shallots and apples to the pan and sauté until brown. Add the wine, chicken broth, vinegar, honey, and mustard.

Return the chicken to the pan, bring to a boil, and simmer gently for 30 minutes. Remove the chicken to a preheated serving platter.

Put the sauce in a blender and blend until smooth. Pour the sauce over the chicken and sprinkle with parsley.

LEMON CHICKEN

SERVES: 4 TO 6

THIS has all the elements of a truly great recipe. It takes minutes to prepare, is easy to make, works as well for one as for six, and wins everyone's favor. I serve it as a wonderful light luncheon dish.

3 whole chicken breasts, skinned, boned, and halved
Juice of 1 lemon
1 teaspoon grated fresh ginger or 1/4 teaspoon ground ginger
1 clove garlic, put through a garlic press
2 tablespoons cornstarch
1 tablespoon vegetable oil
1 tablespoon water
2 tablespoons vegetable oil
1 pound snow peas, cleaned and left in ice water for 5 minutes (or 1 head of broccoli, stem peeled and stem and flowerets cut in medium-size pieces)
Salt and pepper to taste
1 cup condensed chicken broth

Cut the chicken breasts into thin strips. Put them in a bowl and add the lemon juice, ginger, garlic, cornstarch, 1 tablespoon vegetable oil, and water. Mix all these ingredients together and let marinate for about 10 minutes.

Heat the 2 tablespoons vegetable oil in a heavy sauté pan. When the oil is very hot, add the drained snow peas or broccoli, season with salt and pepper, and stir constantly for 2 minutes. Remove vegetables and set aside.

Add marinated chicken breasts to the hot pan, season with salt and pepper, and stir constantly for about 3 minutes. Then add the chicken broth, bring to a boil, add the snow peas or broccoli, combine, and serve.

I originally got this recipe from a friend of mine, Sylvia Lehrer, in the days when we were cooking in her kitchen, making this dish and others for parties of fifty. Life has certainly improved since then! (Sylvia has since opened a cooking school.)

With this chicken, we served herbed rice and Black Beans (page 86). The chicken may be made up to a day ahead.

CHICKEN ANDALUSIA

SERVES: 6

2 frying chickens, cut in eighths
1 12-ounce or 2 6-ounce cans frozen orange juice concentrate
3 cloves garlic, put through a garlic press
4 tablespoons finely chopped fresh parsley
1/2 cup golden raisins
1/2 cup dry sherry
3/4 cup flour
2 teaspoons salt
3 teaspoons paprika
1/4 cup olive oil
6 tablespoons vegetable oil
1/2 cup sherry
1/3 cup slivered, blanched almonds

Place chicken parts in a deep bowl. Combine orange juice, garlic, and parsley and pour it over the chicken. Mix thoroughly so that all pieces are well coated. Marinate overnight in the refrigerator.

The next day, combine raisins and 1/2 cup sherry and set aside.

Remove chicken from marinade and reserve marinade. Season flour with salt and paprika and coat each piece of chicken with it.

Heat olive oil and 3 tablespoons vegetable oil in a large skillet. Brown chicken, a few pieces at a time, in the skillet, adding the remaining 3 tablespoons of vegetable oil as necessary. Remove chicken parts to platter when done.

To the skillet, add the reserved orange juice marinade and 1/2 cup sherry. Stir and heat through until the surface is deglazed.

Put chicken back into the skillet, spooning the sauce over until pieces are covered. Top with almonds and sherry and raisin mixture. Simmer for about 45 minutes before serving.

ROAST DUCK MADAGASCAR

SERVES: 4

THIS is my updated version of the duck I used to serve to Billy Rose. He thought I made the best roast duck in the world. This is simply a perfectly cooked duck, crisp on the outside and juicy on the inside. The gravy should be served on the side. As Mr. Rose used to say, "I want a crispy crust!"

In the 1960s, I learned from living in a tiny apartment with not much of an exhaust fan to put some water in the bottom of the roasting pan to catch the fat as it drips in; when the fat hits a dry roasting pan heated to 375° F. it will burn and smoke. Before I routinely added the water, making this recipe filled my apartment with smoke.

In those days, green peppercorns were unknown to our hemisphere. They certainly have made a great addition to it. Make sure to get a brand that is freeze-dried or packed in water rather than packed in vinegar.

STOCK:
>*1 medium onion, cut in half*
>*1 small stalk celery with leaves*
>*2 carrots, coarsely chopped*
>*2 sprigs parsley*
>*1 bay leaf*
>*5 black peppercorns*
>*1 teaspoon salt*
>*2 cups dry red wine*
>*1 cup water*
>*Duck giblets*

DUCK:
>*3 tablespoons green peppercorns*
>*1 Long Island duckling, about 5 pounds*
>*Salt and pepper to taste*
>*¹/₂ orange, cut in half*
>*1 stalk celery with leaves*
>*¹/₂ onion, cut in half*
>*1 sprig parsley*
>*1 tablespoon softened butter mixed with*
>*1 tablespoon flour*

To make the stock: Put the stock ingredients in a heavy saucepan. Bring to a boil and simmer for 1 hour. Then put the stock through a strainer and add the green peppercorns.

To roast the duck: Preheat oven to 375° F.

Rub the duck inside and out with salt and pepper. Stuff cavity with orange, celery, onion, and parsley and close the opening with a metal skewer.

Put the duck on its back on a rack in a roasting pan. Roast for 1 hour. Pour off the drippings and add the stock. Baste the duck with the stock every 10 minutes for another 45 minutes.

Remove duck from the roasting pan and keep warm. Pour the pan juices into a small saucepan and add the mixed butter and flour. Let it come to a boil and simmer about 5 minutes. Serve gravy on the side.

CHOUCROUTE GARNIE

SERVES: 6

I went back to Austria to learn to ski a few years ago. One of my favorite parts of skiing is coming back from the slopes and having a choucroute garnie, the ultimate après-ski meal. Preparing it used to be my idea of skiing, but now I would have no objection if someone else made it for me while I was skiing. However, I am still a better "après-skier" than a skier.

The kind of sauerkraut you use in this recipe is important. I favor Hengstenberg's, which is made not far from my hometown. Made with wine, it is so delicious that it tastes good even raw. It is carried by many supermarkets and is worth taking some effort to find. If you have a ski lodge, get yourself a case!

3 slices bacon, cut in strips about ¼-inch long
1 onion, finely chopped
2 1-pound, 12-ounce cans sauerkraut
1 golden delicious apple, peeled, cored, and chopped
6 juniper berries
1 bay leaf
1 bottle dry white wine
2 pig's knuckles
1 pound fresh lean pork
1 small smoked butt
4 kassler rippchen (smoked pork chops)
1 kielbasa (sausage)

Sauté the bacon in a heavy saucepan. Add the onion and sauté for 5 minutes.

Add the sauerkraut with its juices, apple, juniper berries, bay leaf, and wine. Mix well and add the pig's knuckles, pork, and smoked butt. Bring to a boil and simmer for 1½ hours. Add the kassler rippchen and kielbasa and simmer for another 20 minutes.

Put the sauerkraut on a flat platter, carve the smoked butt and pork and put around the platter with the rest of the ingredients. Serve with dark bread or steamed potatoes.

CALF'S LIVER
WITH ONIONS
AND APPLES

SERVES: 4

As a little girl, when I was asked to pick my favorite dish to have for lunch on my birthday, this is what I requested. My mother served it with mashed potatoes and watercress salad. It remains my favorite today.

When preparing liver it is important to:

1) use calf's liver;

2) remove all sinews (I learned that from an English nanny in one of the homes in which I worked); and

3) most important—do not overcook. It should be light pink inside.

2 tablespoons safflower oil
1 pound calf's liver, sliced and all sinews removed
Salt and pepper to taste
2 onions, thinly sliced
2 apples, peeled, cored, and thinly sliced
½ cup condensed beef broth
1 tablespoon cider vinegar
1 teaspoon honey
1 teaspoon meat extract (Bovril)
1 teaspoon cornstarch, mixed with
¼ cup water
1 tablespoon finely chopped fresh parsley

Heat the safflower oil in a heavy sauté pan and add the calf's liver. Sauté quickly, no more than 1 minute on each side. Remove the liver from the pan and season it with salt and pepper.

Brown the onions and apples in the sauté pan, adding more oil if necessary. Then add the rest of the ingredients and simmer for about 1 minute.

Return the liver to this sauce and reheat to cook to desired doneness (no more than 1 to 2 minutes).

THE French love monkfish. Luckily for us, they made Americans aware of it. Consequently, it is now very popular here. I love its meaty texture—almost like a fillet of beef. This texture makes it possible to treat it in many different ways, and it is easy to cook. I have found that roasting is the cooking method that works best with this fish.

I used to serve this ginger sauce with fillet of sole. It is also great with the monkfish.

2 scallions
⅓ cup soy sauce
⅓ cup condensed chicken broth
½ teaspoon sugar
⅓ cup water
1 teaspoon cornstarch, mixed with
1 tablespoon water
2 tablespoons corn oil
2 tablespoons finely shredded fresh ginger
3 pounds monkfish
Juice of 1 lemon
Salt and pepper to taste
1 teaspoon corn oil

Preheat oven to 350° F.

Chop the white part of the scallions. (Reserve the green part for decoration, slicing it into julienne strips.)

Mix soy sauce, chicken broth, sugar, and water. Add cornstarch mixed with water.

Heat corn oil in a small saucepan. Add the scallion whites and ginger and cook until light brown. Add soy sauce mixture and bring to a boil. Keep the sauce warm.

Season the monkfish with the lemon juice, salt, and pepper. Rub the fish with a little corn oil. If the fillet has a skinny tail end, tuck it under so that it does not dry up.

Put fish in a roasting pan and roast for 15 to 20 minutes, depending on its thickness. Test the fish by inserting a fork in the thickest part of the fish. It is done when the flesh is white rather than translucent.

Remove fish from the oven, cut it in slices, and put it on a platter. Pour some ginger sauce over it and garnish with the julienned scallion greens.

OPPOSITE: *Monkfish with Ginger Sauce*
(page 73)

Fillet of Sole Joinville (page 76)

Grilled Swordfish with Tomato Sauce
(page 77)

FILLET OF SOLE JOINVILLE

SERVES: 6 TO 10

THE original version of this dish comes from Dione Lucas's *Cooking School Cookbook*, also the source of my Chocolate Normandy recipe. I learned about Dione Lucas while working for Billy Rose, for whom she had previously been chef. She became one of my first heroes in the food business.

This particular recipe provides an example of how the good old days were not so good. When I first made this, with food processors not yet available, I had to put the salmon through a grinder twice and then through a sieve. Then I added the cream drop by drop, using a mixer or, worse, by hand. This involved an hour of work and an hour to clean up afterward. Now the whole process takes all of three minutes.

At your fish store, ask for the skin and bones of your salmon as well as additional fish bones (about a pound altogether) to use for the fish stock.

9 medium-size fillets of sole
½ cup lemon juice

FISH STOCK:
Bones and skins from salmon and sole
1 cup water
2 cups dry white wine
½ onion
½ stalk celery with leaves
1 carrot, cut into 1-inch pieces
2 sprigs fresh dill
1 bay leaf
6 peppercorns
¼ teaspoon salt

SALMON MOUSSE:
1½ pounds salmon, skinned and boned
2 egg whites
1½ cups light cream
2 teaspoons salt
2 shakes of cayenne pepper

VELOUTÉ SAUCE:
4 tablespoons butter
4 tablespoons flour
2 cups strained fish stock
Salt and pepper to taste
½ cup light cream
2 egg yolks mixed with
2 tablespoons sherry
1 bunch watercress for garnish

Generously butter an 8-inch ring mold.

Cut the fillets of sole in half lengthwise, making sure the backbone has been removed. (If you find any bones, save them for the fish stock.) Then wash them in water and lemon juice. Line the ring mold with the fillets, placing them pale side down. They should overlap slightly, with the broader ends hanging over the outer edge of the mold.

To make the fish stock: Put all of the fish stock ingredients in a large, heavy saucepan. Bring slowly to a boil and simmer for 30 minutes. Strain.

To make the salmon mousse: Preheat oven to 350° F.

Put the salmon into a food processor and add the egg whites. Mix for 30 seconds or so. With processor running, add the light cream very slowly. When all the cream has been added, season mixture with the salt and cayenne.

Fill the lined mold with the mousse and fold the ends of the fillets over it. Cover with aluminum foil and stand the mold in a roasting pan. Fill the pan with hot water halfway up the mold and put into the oven for 25 minutes.

To make the velouté sauce: Melt the butter in a heavy saucepan and add the flour. Slowly mix in the strained fish stock, using a small whisk to prevent lumps. Then season with salt and pepper to taste. Add the light cream and simmer for 5 minutes.

Just before serving time, put a little of the sauce into the egg and sherry mixture. Combine and pour into the sauce.

To serve: To unmold the fish, just put your serving platter over the center of the mold and invert; the mold will lift right off. If there is any liquid from the fish, blot it up with paper towels. Pour some of the sauce over the mold and fill center with watercress. Serve with the remaining sauce on the side.

ALTHOUGH this recipe calls for a sauté pan, if you have a grill, this is the time to use it; when you grill swordfish, something magical happens. I, unfortunately, do not possess a grill, so I just enjoy the swordfish sautéed.

Be careful not to overcook the fish.

4 ¹/₂-inch-thick swordfish steaks
Juice of 1 lemon
Salt and pepper to taste
3 tablespoons butter
3 tablespoons olive oil
¹/₂ cup chopped red onion
2 ripe tomatoes, peeled and coarsely chopped
2 tablespoons coarsely chopped fresh coriander
2 tablespoons capers
¹/₂ cup heavy cream
Fresh coriander (or chopped fresh parsley) for garnish

GRILLED SWORDFISH WITH TOMATO SAUCE

SERVES: 4

Sprinkle the lemon juice over the swordfish. Season with salt and pepper.

In a heavy sauté pan, heat the butter and olive oil. Sauté the swordfish steaks for 3 minutes on each side. Remove them from the pan and keep them warm.

To the same pan, add the red onion and sauté for about 2 minutes. Add tomatoes, coriander, capers, and salt and pepper to taste. Combine well and cook for 2 minutes—just enough to heat through.

Add the heavy cream. Let it come to a boil.

Pour sauce over swordfish steaks. Garnish with coriander or chopped parsley.

SAUTEED ALMOND SOLE

SERVES: 6

WITH its delicious pairing of the crispy almonds with the tender fish, this recipe wins hands down over the bread-crumb treatment of sole.

This is one of the few times when I sauté a fish rather than broil or bake it. This is not a good dish to make when serving more than six people, as the fish should be served immediately. However, as noted below, the uncooked fillets may be prepared several hours ahead.

6 fillets of sole, flounder, or fluke
¼ cup fresh lemon juice
Salt and pepper to taste
1 cup flour
3 egg whites, lightly beaten
2 cups finely chopped almonds
4 tablespoons butter
¼ cup vegetable oil
Fresh lemon, cut into wedges, for garnish

Sprinkle the fillets with lemon juice and season them with salt and pepper. Dip them in the flour, shaking to remove any excess. (They should be merely dusted.) Next, dip them in the egg whites on both sides and then in the almonds, patting to cover well. Remove to a rack or waxed paper and allow to dry for at least 10 minutes. (You may do this several hours ahead of time, keeping the fillets in the refrigerator on a cookie sheet covered with waxed paper.)

Heat butter and oil in a heavy sauté pan. As soon as it is very hot, add the fillets, making sure they do not touch one another, and cook for 1 or 2 minutes on each side, or until they are nicely browned.

Serve with wedges of fresh lemon and a green salad.

SIDE DISHES

WHEN buying broccoli, make sure the tops are entirely dark green, in no way yellow. Spike Vegetable Seasoning, a combination of herbs and spices, is available in health-food stores. I use it often with vegetables.

1 head broccoli
2 tablespoons vegetable oil
¼ cup water
About 1 tablespoon Spike Vegetable Seasoning
Salt and pepper to taste
3 tablespoons pine nuts, lightly toasted

Remove flowerets from broccoli stem and break into even sizes. Peel stem with a paring knife to remove the hard outer fiber. Cut stem on an angle into even slices.

Heat vegetable oil in a sauté pan and add the broccoli. Stir until pan is hot again. Add ¼ cup water. Cover immediately and let steam for 3 minutes. Then turn off the heat, but keep pan covered for a few more minutes.

Just before serving, season with Spike Seasoning and salt and pepper. Sprinkle with toasted pine nuts.

BROCCOLI WITH PINE NUTS

SERVES: 4

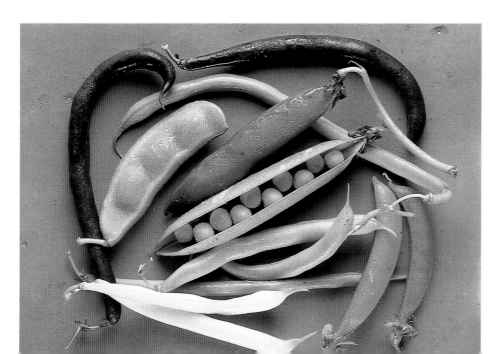

Here is a selection of peas and beans (clockwise from lower right): sugar snaps, wax beans, lima beans, purple and green string beans, and, in the center, peas—all of which make a variety of useful side dishes, such as Green Beans with Shallots (page 128)

STIR-FRIED ASPARAGUS

SERVES: 4

I always peel my asparagus, to a point half an inch below the tip, before cooking. It tastes sweeter and cooks more quickly. The cooked asparagus should still be crunchy.

1 pound asparagus, the tough ends cut off, peeled, and washed
2 tablespoons vegetable oil
1/4 cup water
1 tablespoon Spike Vegetable Seasoning
1 tablespoon sesame seeds

Cut the asparagus stalks diagonally into 2-inch pieces.

In a heavy sauté pan, heat the oil until it is very hot. Add the asparagus and stir constantly for 1 minute, then add the water. Cover the pan immediately and cook for another 2 to 3 minutes, depending on the thickness of the pieces, shaking the pan occasionally.

Season with Spike Seasoning, sprinkle on sesame seeds, and serve.

WHITE CABBAGE WITH BUTTER

SERVES: 6

THIS is a recipe from my first cookbook, which I wrote back in 1968, and it is as delicious today as it was then.

1 head white cabbage
1/2 cup (1 stick) butter
1/4 cup water
Salt and pepper to taste

Preheat oven to 350° F.

Remove the outer leaves of the cabbage and cut into quarters. Remove the center core and shred the cabbage into medium-fine slices, as you would for coleslaw. (This can be done in the food processor.)

Butter a fairly deep, large casserole or baking dish and pour the water into it. Add a layer of cabbage. Sprinkle with salt and pepper and dot with small pieces of butter. Repeat making layers until all the cabbage has been used, saving a little butter for the top.

Cover tightly with a lid or aluminum foil and bake for approximately 30 minutes. Serve immediately.

AT the time I was executive chef in the dining room of *Gourmet* magazine, I had the occasion to cook for many of its advertising clients. Among them were the publishers of *Tastes of Liberty* (New York: Stewart, Tabori & Chang, 1985), which was published for the centennial of the Statue of Liberty.

I was asked to prepare this recipe from their cookbook for lunch as an appetizer, and I enjoyed it so much that I now serve it hot instead of ratatouille. Like ratatouille, it may be served as a meal in itself, and it makes a great side dish, particularly with lamb.

Caponata can easily be made the day before and reheated.

CAPONATA

SERVES: 4 TO 6

1 small eggplant, cut into ¹/₂-inch cubes
2 teaspoons coarse salt
1 large red or green bell pepper, seeded and cut into 1-inch dice
1 large yellow bell pepper, seeded and cut into 1-inch dice
¹/₂ cup coarsely chopped onion
¹/₄ cup coarsely chopped celery
¹/₄ cup olive oil
1 1-pound can Italian plum tomatoes, drained and seeded
2 medium zucchini, cut into ¹/₄-inch slices
2 tablespoons pine nuts
2 tablespoons tomato paste
1 to 2 tablespoons white wine vinegar
1 tablespoon sugar
6 large green olives, pitted and sliced thinly
1 bay leaf
¹/₈ teaspoon black pepper

Place eggplant in colander and sprinkle with the salt. Cover with a heavy plate and drain for 30 minutes.

Sauté peppers, onion, and celery in 2 tablespoons of the oil in a large sauté pan over medium heat, stirring frequently until the onions are soft, about 5 to 8 minutes. Remove from skillet and set aside. Add remaining oil to sauté pan.

Squeeze excess liquid from eggplant. Sauté over medium heat, stirring frequently, until lightly browned, about 5 to 8 minutes. Return pepper and onion mixture to pan and stir in all remaining ingredients. Cook over medium-low heat, stirring frequently, until most of the liquid has evaporated, about 10 to 15 minutes.

Serve hot or cold.

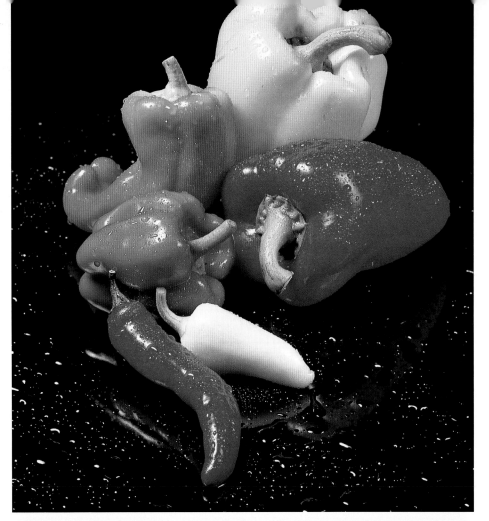

This collection of peppers includes yellow, red, and green bell peppers, hot chili and jalapeño peppers, and a mild Italian frying pepper

Stir-fried Asparagus (page 80)

OPPOSITE: *Caponata (page 81)*

82

CARROTS WITH GRAPES

SERVES: 6

NOW that fresh baby carrots are easy to find, use them when you can get them. Otherwise, peel regular carrots and cut them into 1-inch diagonal slices.

The grapes are simply heated rather than cooked so that they will keep their nice shape.

2 pounds whole baby carrots (or 2 bunches regular carrots)
½ cup water
3 tablespoons butter
2 tablespoons maple sugar (or maple syrup)
½ pound seedless red or green grapes
2 tablespoons chopped fresh parsley for garnish

If using regular carrots, cut as directed above. Simmer carrots in water until tender, about 5 to 7 minutes. Drain any water that remains.

In a large saucepan, melt butter. Add maple sugar or syrup and drained carrots. Combine well, heating carrots through again. Add grapes. Keep on heat for another 2 minutes, stirring constantly.

Just before serving, sprinkle with parsley.

CRACKED WHEAT

SERVES: 4

BESIDES serving this as a side dish, I also eat it topped with fresh steamed vegetables for dinner, and I often add it to a salad.

2 tablespoons butter (or olive oil)
1 medium onion, chopped
½ cup chopped celery
1 cup bulgur (cracked wheat)
2 cups condensed chicken broth
Salt and pepper to taste

In a saucepan, heat butter or olive oil. Add onion and celery. Sauté without browning for about 3 minutes. Add bulgur wheat, chicken broth, salt, and pepper. Combine well and bring to a boil.

Reduce heat to simmer, cover, and continue cooking for 15 minutes. Turn off heat and let sit for 5 minutes before serving.

MANY people are unfamiliar with this grain, which is very easy to make. This recipe is wonderful served with Marinated Leg of Lamb (page 62) during the summer. (In winter, I have Potatoes Provençale with the lamb.)

Like cracked wheat, couscous is also good with steamed fresh vegetables. If you have any left over, put it in your salad the next day. It tastes great.

NOTE: If you use water instead of the chicken broth, add some salt to taste.

COUSCOUS

SERVES: 6

2 tablespoons vegetable oil
½ red pepper, cut into small cubes
½ yellow pepper, cut into small cubes
4 scallions, thinly sliced
½ cup currants
3 cups water (or chicken broth)
½ teaspoon turmeric
2 cups couscous
2 tablespoons chopped fresh parsley for garnish

Heat the vegetable oil in a saucepan. Add the peppers and scallions and sauté for about 2 minutes. Add the currants, water or chicken broth, and turmeric. Combine well and let it come to a boil.

Add the couscous and stir. Cover the pan and turn off the heat. Let sit for about 10 minutes. Then fluff the couscous with a fork and serve with parsley sprinkled over the top. For a special presentation, place in timbale molds and unmold onto the plate.

SAFFRON Rissotto is the perfect accompaniment to Osso Bucco (page 62). I also sometimes serve this with veal.

SAFFRON RISSOTTO

SERVES: 8

2 cans condensed chicken broth
2 cans water
4 tablespoons olive oil
½ cup chopped onion
2 cups Arborio rice
¼ teaspoon powdered saffron or 1 teaspoon threads of saffron

Bring chicken broth and water to a boil and keep simmering.

In a heavy sauté pan, heat olive oil and add onion. Sauté for 5 minutes without letting the onion brown. Stir in the rice and cook for another 2 minutes. Add saffron and boiling chicken broth. Bring to a boil again and turn down the heat. Simmer, covered, until most of the liquid has been absorbed, about 30 minutes.

BLACK BEANS

SERVES: 6

THIS recipe is especially good with Chicken Andalusia (page 69). It is a particularly spicy and attractive dish.

Note that it must be started a day ahead. In fact, the entire recipe may be made ahead and reheated. If, on the other hand, you prefer to make it the same day, bring the beans to a boil in a large pot of water at a level about 2 inches above the beans and simmer for 5 minutes. Turn off the heat and let beans sit for one hour, then proceed with the recipe.

1 pound dried black beans
1 green pepper, cut in half, cored, and seeded
1 medium onion, cut in half
3 tablespoons olive oil
2 green peppers, diced
2 onions, chopped
3 cloves garlic, minced
1 bay leaf
¼ teaspoon cumin powder
1 teaspoon wine vinegar
½ cup dry red wine
1 8-ounce can tomato sauce

Soak beans overnight in water at a level three inches above the beans, adding 1 green pepper and 1 onion, both cut in half.

The next day, drain beans, place in a saucepan with fresh water to cover, returning the pepper and onion, and bring to a boil. Cook over medium heat for 1½ hours.

Heat the oil in a skillet. Sauté the rest of the peppers and onions in the skillet until the onions are limp. Add garlic to onion mixture and cook for 1 minute more. Add remaining ingredients and simmer for 10 minutes.

Add the vegetable mixture to the cooked beans and stir through. Simmer for 45 minutes.

DESSERTS

🍃

A LTHOUGH these days it seems that everyone is on a diet of one kind or another, I have not seen any impact in my dining room, where I always serve a sampling of four different desserts, and rarely a plate returns to the kitchen that has not been cleaned. This may be because most people don't eat desserts on a daily basis, so when they go out or entertain they decide to splurge and look forward to it. Another explanation may be that my desserts are particularly good. In fact, my Chocolate Normandy has won me a lot of goodwill with bankers and everyone else.

I firmly believe that nothing you eat is bad for you, provided you eat it in moderation. So, if you like desserts, enjoy them. We all need now and then that feel-good sensation they give us.

All gelatin-based desserts, such as mousses and cold soufflés, may be made up to two days ahead of time. After that, they turn rubbery. Sorbets can be made as far ahead as a week.

Chocolate Normandy (page 92)

LEMON MOUSSE WITH RASPBERRY SAUCE

SERVES: 12

THE difference between a lemon soufflé and a lemon mousse is only in the presentation. In the case of a soufflé, I fasten a collar around the dish to extend the height, making the lemon mousse/soufflé appear to be rising above the dish (see directions on page 89). When I serve this as a mousse, I simply pour it into a large bowl.

This recipe serves 12, but you may cut it in half for a smaller group when serving it as a mousse. When serving it as a soufflé, make it in the specified amount.

I often served this recipe in the executive dining room at *Gourmet* magazine.

2 packages unflavored gelatin, dissolved in
Juice of 1 lemon
1 cup sugar
8 eggs
½ cup fresh lemon juice
2 cups heavy cream, whipped to soft peaks
Raspberry Sauce (page 115)
Fresh raspberries for garnish

To dissolve the gelatin, sprinkle it over the juice of one lemon in a small heatproof dish. Put dish in a pan with an inch or two of boiling water. Gelatin is dissolved when it is clear rather than cloudy looking. Allow it to cool slightly.

Beat sugar and eggs with an electric mixer on high speed for about 10 minutes, until light and creamy. With mixer at high speed, add dissolved gelatin slowly. Lower speed and add lemon juice, blending only a few seconds longer.

Fold in whipped cream by hand. Pour into a large bowl and freeze for 2 to 3 hours.

At serving time, scoop out individual portions, placing each on a plate and surrounding it with a pool of Raspberry Sauce and topping with fresh raspberries.

WHITE CHOCOLATE MOUSSE

SERVES: 12

WHITE chocolate mousse is a fairly new creation, which became chic one or two seasons ago. The Tobler people called me at one time to ask me to develop a recipe for them, and this is what my chef, Walter, came up with. It is wonderful and easy to make, but don't serve it to real chocoholics—they want the dark stuff.

I sometimes swirl this into regular chocolate mousse to make a black-and-white mousse. (You can have a really good time playing with this.) I also serve this with Raspberry Sauce (page 115) and fresh raspberries.

1 cup heavy cream
3 egg yolks
28 ounces white chocolate, grated
3 cups heavy cream, whipped

Candied violets (or fresh raspberries and fresh mint)

Combine the heavy cream and egg yolks well with a whisk and heat gently over very low heat until it starts to get thick, making sure it does not come to a boil.

Remove pan from heat and stand pot in a basin of cold water to lower the heat slightly. Add grated chocolate and stir until melted and smooth. Allow mixture to cool.

Fold in the whipped cream. Pour into a large serving bowl or individual serving bowls and chill for at least 5 hours, preferably overnight.

Garnish with candied violets or raspberries and mint leaves.

BECAUSE everyone loves frozen soufflés, I try to think of unusual variations of this dessert. I like to serve this recipe in the fall or winter when chestnuts are in season. However, now that chestnut puree comes packed in cans, making this recipe is no longer a big production.

CHESTNUT SOUFFLÉ

SERVES: 12

2 packages unflavored gelatin
¹⁄₄ cup light rum
¹⁄₂ cup sugar
8 eggs
1 cup sweetened chestnut puree, thinned with
2 tablespoons rum
2 cups heavy cream, whipped to soft peaks

GARNISH:

Whipped cream
Candied chestnuts

Fasten a waxed-paper collar that rises at least 2 inches above the rim around the outside of a 1½-quart soufflé dish with cotton string. Oil the paper lightly to make it easier to put around the dish.

Sprinkle the gelatin over the rum in a small heatproof dish. Put dish in a pan with an inch or two of boiling water. Gelatin is dissolved when it is clear rather than cloudy looking. Allow it to cool slightly.

Beat the sugar and eggs with an electric mixer on high speed for 10 to 15 minutes, until mixture is very fluffy. With mixer running, add the dissolved gelatin very slowly to the egg mixture.

Fold in the chestnut puree and the whipped cream by hand. Pour into soufflé dish and freeze for at least 2 hours.

At serving time, remove the paper collar and decorate with whipped cream and candied chestnuts.

FRANGELICO SOUFFLÉ

SERVES: 12

I love the flavor of hazelnuts, and their taste is wonderful in this soufflé. I generally make a praline of sugar and hazelnuts, breaking the praline into large chunks for decoration or pulverizing it in the food processor for an extra crunch in the soufflé. More than ¼ cup of the praline will make the soufflé too sweet.

2 packages unflavored gelatin
¼ cup water
½ cup sugar
8 eggs
½ cup Frangelico liqueur
2 cups heavy cream, whipped to soft peaks
¼ cup (or less) praline powder, optional

GARNISH:
Whipped cream
Praline pieces
Fresh mint

Fasten a waxed-paper collar around a 1½-quart soufflé dish (see directions on page 89).

Sprinkle gelatin over water in a small heatproof dish. Put dish into a small pan with a couple of inches of boiling water. Gelatin is dissolved when mixture is clear rather than cloudy.

Beat the sugar and eggs with an electric mixer on high speed for about 10 minutes, until mixture is light and creamy. With mixer running, add the dissolved gelatin very slowly to the egg mixture. Then add the liqueur slowly to the egg mixture.

Fold in the whipped cream and the praline powder, if used, by hand. Pour into the soufflé dish and freeze for at least 2 hours.

At serving time, remove the paper collar and decorate the soufflé with whipped cream squeezed through a pastry bag, pieces of the praline, and fresh mint leaves.

PRALINE:
1 cup sugar
¼ cup chopped hazelnuts

Melt the sugar in a heavy skillet over medium heat until it is caramel-colored, taking care not to burn it, then add the hazelnuts, mixing them well with the caramel. Pour onto oiled aluminum foil in a jelly roll pan to cool.

A dessert quartet (clockwise from top):
*Chocolate Normandy (page 92), Coeur
à la Crème (page 129), Caramel-
glazed Apple Tart (page 140), and
Frangelico Soufflé*

CHOCOLATE NORMANDY

SERVES: 12

I have told this story about my Chocolate Normandy to thousands of people, but since it has gotten me so many things worth having in life, and since everyone truly loves this story, here I go again.

In 1965, I had gone to an employment agency looking for a job as a chef. I was twenty-one and had very little in the way of credentials or experience as a chef in America, but I had a fierce determination to bluff it through. At the time, Billy Rose had commissioned this agency to find him a new chef. I knew he was somebody important, but I wasn't sure why.

I applied for the job and, surprisingly, was given an appointment for an interview. In the meantime, I asked everyone about Billy Rose. Somebody mentioned his book *Wine, Women, and Words*. I went to the public library and read every word carefully over and over until I felt I knew all about him.

The day of the interview I was intoxicated by my own self-confidence. I was going to conquer the great Billy Rose! I was brought into his presence by the butler and was a little surprised by his small size; from his story I had imagined him to be six feet tall. "You're a gourmet chef?" he asked incredulously. I was a little shaken, but I replied coolly, "You can't judge a book by its cover, Mr. Rose."

He liked that, I guess, because he didn't have me thrown out. He asked me several questions about cookery, some about salary (being a millionaire didn't make him overly generous), and finally asked, "Can you make Chocolate Mousse Normandy?"

"Of course," I replied.

"What's your recipe?" he asked.

"Mr. Rose," I rejoined, "I make it a policy to give my recipes to no one." Whereupon he hired me and told me to report in three days.

It was not until I had walked in a daze for some blocks that I realized that I had never heard of Chocolate Mousse Normandy. I rushed home to my sizable collection of cookbooks to find it. It was not there. Frantically, I called friends, chefs, magazines. I couldn't sleep. I thought maybe Billy Rose was playing a cruel joke on me.

Finally, on the third day, in desperation, I went to the New York Public Library on Forty-second Street. I leafed through every cookbook on the shelves. And finally, I found it—in one of Dione Lucas's books. (I discovered later that she had once worked for Mr. Rose.) It was a moment of tremendous relief. I made it for Mr. Rose the first night and have been making it ever since, with a few variations of my own.

Although this recipe calls for a lot of work, it is worth it, and the cake can be done well ahead and kept in the freezer for a week.

For this truly top-of-the-line in chocolate desserts, it pays to use the finest-quality ingredients. Who knows what you might not be able to get with it?

¾ pound bittersweet chocolate
¾ cup light rum
¾ cup (1½ sticks) butter, at room temperature
½ cup confectioners' sugar
4 egg yolks
½ cup salted almonds, finely ground
4 egg whites

¼ cup confectioners' sugar
½ vanilla bean, seeds only
2 cups heavy cream

GARNISH:
½ cup heavy cream, whipped with 1 tablespoon confectioners' sugar
2 packages chocolate cat tongues, preferably Feodora brand
Satin ribbon and a fresh flower
Mocha beans

Cut a circle of waxed paper to fit exactly the bottom of an 8-inch springform pan. Line the sides with waxed paper, putting a little butter on the mold so that the paper stays on.

Break the chocolate into small pieces and melt it, together with the rum, in a small, heavy pan over low heat, stirring constantly. When the chocolate is melted, take it off the heat and cool, but do not let it set.

With an electric mixer on high speed, cream the butter until light and fluffy, then add ½ cup confectioners' sugar and beat well. Add the egg yolks, one at a time, the almonds, and, finally, the cooled chocolate.

In another bowl, beat the egg whites. When they form soft peaks, add ¼ cup confectioners' sugar and vanilla seeds, then continue beating until the mixture is stiff but not dry. Fold this into the chocolate mixture until well combined.

Whip the 2 cups heavy cream until stiff and fold it into the chocolate and egg-white mixture, combining it well without overmixing. Pour this mixture into the prepared mold. Cover with plastic wrap and freeze for at least 2 hours or overnight. (In fact, it can be frozen for several days.)

To serve, open the mold and remove the waxed paper. Put the Normandy upside down on a silver serving tray and remove the circle of waxed paper. Then put the cat tongues around the sides close together. Wrap a satin ribbon around the middle of the cat tongues, make a bow, and put a fresh flower in the bow. Decorate the top with whipped cream and candy mocha beans if you have them.

PLUM TART

SERVES: 12

IN Germany, this tart is traditionally made with a yeast dough, but I don't have the patience to wait for a yeast dough. Anyway, I like this crust better, because I like a thin crust—it is simply a vessel to hold the fruit.

This tart ideally is made in the afternoon and served slightly warm. Once it is refrigerated, it isn't the same. However, the crust may be made and the plums macerated the night before. Just assemble and bake it a few hours before you plan to serve it.

CRUST:

> *2 cups flour*
> *½ cup (1 stick) butter, cut in pieces*
> *¼ cup shortening, preferably Crisco brand*
> *¼ cup hazelnuts, chopped*
> *⅓ cup ice water*

FILLING:

> *2½ pounds prune plums, pitted and quartered, skins left on*
> *¼ cup superfine sugar*
> *2 tablespoons cornstarch*

TOPPING:

> *¼ cup sugar*
> *1 tablespoon cinnamon*
> *½ cup hazelnuts, chopped*

To make the crust: In a food processor, combine the flour, butter, shortening, and hazelnuts. Process for 30 seconds, then add ice water through the top while the processor is running. Continue processing until dough forms a ball. Remove, wrap in waxed paper, and refrigerate for 30 minutes.

Roll out dough. Place in a 10- or 12-inch tart pan.

Preheat oven to 375° F.

To make the filling: While the dough is resting, cut plums into quarters and place in a bowl. Mix superfine sugar and cornstarch. Sprinkle over fruit and macerate for 10 minutes.

To assemble: Place plums close together in rows on the crust. Pour juices evenly over the plums. Sprinkle ¼ cup sugar, cinnamon, and chopped hazelnuts over plums.

Bake for 35 minutes or until desired color (I prefer it lightly browned) is achieved.

Ripe peaches, plums, and apricots make a number of wonderful desserts

OPPOSITE: *Fresh Fruit Kabobs (page 96)*

FRESH FRUIT KABOBS

FOR this recipe, the ingredients may vary, depending on the availability of the fruit. You can put just about anything on these skewers. Just think in terms of colors and textures—the presentation is what makes this recipe so much fun.

This is certainly a dessert that lends itself perfectly to a buffet. The fruit doesn't get mushy as it does in a fruit salad.

NOTE: I always arrange the kabobs on top of ti leaves, which can be purchased in a flower shop.

Fresh strawberries, washed, dried, and hulled
Kiwi fruit, peeled and cut into quarters
Fresh cantaloupe, skin removed, seeded, and cut into chunks
Fresh pineapple, peeled, cored, and cut into chunks
Fresh honeydew, skin removed, seeded, and cut into chunks
6-inch bamboo skewers

GARNISH:
Ti leaves (see NOTE*)*
Fresh flower

Skewer the fruits in the same order as they appear on the ingredient list.

Wash ti leaves with cold water and dry them. Arrange in a circular fan pattern. Arrange skewers on the leaves, side by side, and put a fresh flower in the middle.

POACHED PEARS IN WINE

SERVES: 6

THIS is still one of the great classic desserts. The pears may be served plain, or with a raspberry (page 115), hot chocolate (page 115), or a butterscotch sauce. If you serve the pears with vanilla ice cream and hot chocolate sauce, you have Pears Hélène.

NOTE: This syrup can be used to poach pears, apples, oranges, or any other fruit you wish. You may replace the vanilla bean with 1 cinnamon stick, 3 cloves, and the peel of 1 orange.

2 cups white wine
2 cups water
1 to 1½ cups sugar, depending on the sweetness of the fruit
1 whole vanilla bean
6 pears, peeled

Put the wine, water, sugar, and vanilla bean in a saucepan over medium heat. Bring to a boil, stirring occasionally, and simmer this syrup for 10 minutes.

Put the pears into the syrup and poach them over gentle heat for about 10 to 20 minutes, covered. Test doneness by putting the point of a knife into the pear. There should be no resistance. The timing depends on the size and ripeness of the pears.

Cool the pears in the syrup, then remove them. Arrange in a glass bowl and serve plain or with your choice of sauce.

ONE of the things I learned very early in life is that in order to get people to do things for you, it helps to flatter them. Flattery does get you almost anywhere, and there is nothing more flattering than having a dish created and named after you.

The lawyer this recipe was created and named for was far too expensive for me at the time. I could never have afforded his counsel if it were not for my great lunches and this Peaches Advocate. So keep this in mind the next time you need something important.

You may make these peaches ahead of time and put them in the oven when your guests arrive.

For another variation, crumble an Amaretto cookie over each peach half in place of the honey and sesame seeds.

6 ripe peaches, peeled, cut in half, and pits removed
6 teaspoons honey
1/2 cup cognac
2 tablespoons sesame seeds
1 cup heavy cream
2 tablespoons confectioners' sugar

Preheat oven to 350° F.

Place the peach halves in an ovenproof serving dish. Fill each peach cavity with 1 teaspoon honey, pour the cognac over the peaches, and sprinkle the sesame seeds on top. Cover the dish with aluminum foil and bake for 20 minutes.

Combine heavy cream and confectioners' sugar and whip until very soft, but not stiff, peaks form.

Serve peaches warm with softly whipped cream on the side.

PEACHES ADVOCATE

SERVES: 6

PEACH COBBLER

SERVES: 8

A cobbler is a truly American dessert. I learned all about fruit cobblers from Jacqueline Kennedy, and I used to make them frequently when we were in Hyannis Port. It is simply the best of fresh fruit in season with a biscuit dough on top.

You may use many different kinds of fruit: blueberry or rhubarb combined with strawberry, for example, taste wonderful. Just adjust the sugar according to the sweetness of the fruit.

FILLING:
3 pounds peaches, peeled, pitted, and cut into thick slices
½ cup superfine sugar
3 tablespoons cornstarch
2 tablespoons cognac, peach schnapps, or apple juice

TOP CRUST:
2 cups sifted flour
½ teaspoon salt
2 tablespoons double-acting baking powder
4 tablespoons butter
4 tablespoons shortening, preferably Crisco brand
½ cup milk
½ cup heavy cream
1 teaspoon pure vanilla extract
2 tablespoons melted butter
1½ cups heavy cream, lightly whipped

To make the filling: Combine the peaches, sugar, cornstarch, and cognac or apple juice in a heatproof glass baking dish 9 inches square and 1¾ inches deep. Let sit for about 30 minutes to macerate.

In the meantime, make the crust.

To make the crust: Preheat oven to 450° F.

Put the flour into a food processor. Add the salt and baking powder and process for 20 seconds. Add the butter and shortening and process until well combined, achieving the texture of cornmeal.

Combine milk, cream, and vanilla extract. Pour into processor and process for about 30 seconds.

To assemble: Put the dough on a floured board and roll it out to the size of the baking dish. Place the dough on top of the fruit. Brush with the melted butter. Bake for about 30 to 35 minutes.

Serve while still warm with lightly whipped cream on the side.

IN my dining room, I serve sorbets as a course between the fish and the main course. Whenever I make them, I always use fresh ingredients—the best of what is in season. I do not make my sorbets very sweet, as they are meant to cleanse the palate.

Champagne sorbet and lemon sorbet are two classics that are always elegant and easy to do. Cranberry sorbet is nice to serve at Thanksgiving as a break from cranberry sauce. Sometimes I combine sorbets, serving, for instance, half cranberry and half pear or half champagne and half strawberry.

I like to add fruit brandies to my fruit sorbets. It enhances the flavor even more and gives the sorbets a nicer consistency, since the alcohol prevents the sorbet from freezing rock hard. You might add strawberry schnapps or kirsch to strawberry sorbet, cranberry liqueur to cranberry sorbet, or Williams Pear brandy to pear sorbet. Just be sure you do not add too much, or the sorbet will not freeze. It also will not freeze properly if you add too much sugar, and if you add too little sugar it will freeze too hard. It is a rather delicate balance.

Since there is no lemon fruit brandy that I know of, I always make lemon sorbet on the day I am serving it. If I make it any further in advance, it freezes too hard.

The strawberry sorbet method (page 101) should be used for delicate fresh fruit such as raspberries, blueberries, blackberries, and kiwi fruit. The method for pear sorbet (page 101) should be used for such fruits as peaches, papaya, mango, and pineapple.

You may keep the sorbet in serving glasses in the freezer for up to 30 minutes before serving; beyond that, it gets too hard. Otherwise, serve in chilled glasses.

Four luscious sorbets (clockwise from top): *kiwi (page 101), lemon (page 100), cranberry (page 100), and pear (page 101)*

CHAMPAGNE SORBET

SERVES: 12

2 cups sugar
2 cups water
½ bottle champagne
1 egg white
Fresh mint for garnish

Combine sugar and water in a saucepan. Let come to a boil over medium heat. Simmer until sugar is dissolved, then allow syrup to cool.

Pour syrup into a large bowl. Pour champagne into bowl and stir well.

Beat egg white until stiff peaks form. Add to champagne mixture and combine well.

Transfer the sorbet mixture to an ice-cream maker and follow the manufacturer's directions. If you do not have an ice-cream maker, pour the mixture into a food processor or blender and blend until smooth. Put into a freezerproof glass pie plate or bowl, cover with plastic wrap, and place in freezer until it is hard. Just before serving, return it to the food processor and process until smooth.

At serving time, decorate with mint.

LEMON SORBET

SERVES: 6 TO 8

2 cups water
1 cup sugar
½ cup fresh lemon juice
Grated rind of 1 lemon

Put the water and sugar in a saucepan and bring to a boil over medium heat. Simmer until sugar is dissolved. Remove from heat, add the lemon juice and grated rind. Put the mixture into a shallow bowl to cool.

Transfer the sorbet mixture into an ice-cream maker and follow the manufacturer's directions or proceed as directed above.

CRANBERRY SORBET

SERVES: 20

3 12-ounce packages fresh cranberries
2 quarts water
2 cups granulated sugar
Juice of 3 lemons
½ cup cranberry liqueur

Put all ingredients except cranberry liqueur in a saucepan, bring to a boil, and simmer for 15 minutes. Cool, then put through a blender.

Strain through a fine sieve to discard the skins. Cool the mixture completely. Add the cranberry liqueur.

Transfer the sorbet mixture into an ice-cream maker and follow the manufacturer's directions or proceed as directed above.

1 cup water
³/₄ cup sugar
2 pints fresh strawberries, washed, dried, and cut in half
¹/₄ cup strawberry schnapps or kirsch, optional

Put the water and sugar in a saucepan and bring to a boil over medium heat. Simmer until sugar is dissolved.

Cool the syrup for about 5 minutes and pour over the strawberries in a bowl. (Cooked strawberries lose their color and get mushy.) Let them sit in the syrup for about 30 minutes.

Pour mixture into a food processor or blender and, if you wish, add the schnapps or kirsch. Blend until smooth.

Transfer the sorbet mixture into an ice-cream maker and follow the manufacturer's directions or proceed as directed on page 100.

STRAWBERRY SORBET

SERVES: 4

I N fall, when fresh pears are abundant, this is one of my favorite sorbets. I always add pear brandy for extra flavor.

1 cup water
³/₄ cup sugar
1-inch section of a vanilla bean
4 pears, peeled, cored, and cut into cubes
1 tablespoon Williams Pear Brandy, optional

Combine the water, sugar, and vanilla bean in a saucepan. Bring to a boil, stirring constantly until the sugar is dissolved. Then add the pears, bring to a boil again, cover, and simmer over low heat until the pears are soft. (Test with the point of a knife—there should be no resistance—since the cooking time depends on the ripeness of the pears.)

Cool the mixture and remove the vanilla bean. Pour the mixture into a food processor or blender and, if you wish, add the brandy. Blend until smooth.

Transfer the sorbet mixture into an ice-cream maker and follow the manufacturer's directions or proceed as directed on page 100.

PEAR SORBET

SERVES: 6

A trio of chocolate treats (from top): *Gianduja, Fudge Brownies (page 143), and Truffles*

TRUFFLES

YIELD: ABOUT 2 DOZEN

I consider truffles the ultimate sinfulness in chocolate. I was once asked by a company for advice on how to promote its cognac. I advised them to make truffles with the cognac and to give people a taste and the recipe. To me, cognac and truffles go together like salt and pepper.

The company liked the idea but could not come up with anyone to make the truffles for it. I wound up making thousands of truffles in my kitchen. All my commercial refrigerators were filled from top to bottom, and my house literally oozed chocolate.

I don't advise making thousands, but do make some for yourself and for friends. They make wonderful Christmas presents—and terrific bribes. They can be made several days ahead and kept in the refrigerator.

Serve these confections with after-dinner coffee. Take a bite of the truffle and then a sip of coffee—heaven!

NOTE: Instead of cognac, you may use any kind of liqueur. Grand Marnier and Frangelico give excellent results.

TRUFFLES:
> *³/₄ cup heavy cream*
> *¹/₄ cup cognac (or liqueur)*
> *4 tablespoons (¹/₂ stick) butter*
> *1 pound bittersweet or semisweet chocolate, cut into small pieces*

COATING:
> *¹/₂ cup cocoa powder, preferably imported*
> *¹/₄ cup confectioners' sugar*

Combine all truffle ingredients in a heavy saucepan or the top of a double boiler. Place saucepan over low heat; melt chocolate, stirring ingredients occasionally. When chocolate is melted, remove from heat and cool until mixture begins to thicken. (For best results, place saucepan in ice water and stir constantly.)

When cool, whip mixture with an electric beater on high speed until chocolate is light and fluffy (a creamy beige color), about 10 to 15 minutes.

Using two teaspoons, put small scoops of chocolate on a cookie sheet lined with waxed paper. Place sheet in refrigerator.

Combine coating ingredients in a strainer and sift into a bowl. Dip each truffle into the cocoa mixture, roll it between your hands to coat it, and return it to the cookie sheet. (Make sure your hands are cool, otherwise the truffles will melt.) Refrigerate.

When firm, transfer truffles to a tightly covered container and keep refrigerated until ready to serve.

GIANDUJA

YIELD: ABOUT 30 PIECES

THIS is also sinful stuff, but I only make it at Christmastime. It, too, makes wonderful Christmas presents when packaged attractively. It, too, tastes superlative with espresso after dinner.

I use Toblerone brand milk chocolate, since it contains almonds, which gives it a wonderful texture.

NOTE: Praline paste can be bought in fine gourmet shops or through mail-order sources.

> *1¹/₂ pounds bittersweet chocolate, cut into small pieces*
> *1¹/₂ pounds praline paste*
> *1 pound Toblerone milk chocolate, cut into small pieces*
> *¹/₂ pound praline paste (see NOTE)*

Line a small brownie pan, about 6½ by 8 by 2 inches, with waxed paper.

Melt the bittersweet chocolate over low heat in a heavy saucepan or in a double boiler. Add 1½ pounds praline paste and stir until the chocolate and praline paste are well combined. Pour half of this mixture into the lined brownie pan and cool in the refrigerator.

Meanwhile, in another saucepan or double boiler, melt the Toblerone over low heat, then add ½ pound praline paste, mixing until well combined. Allow this mixture to cool for a while, then pour it on top of the bittersweet chocolate mixture in the brownie pan.

Let the mixture cool in the refrigerator for a while, until it begins to set. Then pour the rest of the bittersweet chocolate mixture on top of it. Cover and let this cool in the refrigerator until hard.

Remove candy from pan by inverting pan; the gianduja should fall right out in a solid block. Cut it into small squares.

BLACK FOREST TORTE

SERVES: 16

COMING from the southern part of Germany, as I do, Black Forest Torte is to me what strawberry shortcake is to a Southern girl in the United States.

I frequently vary this recipe, adding extra chocolate or using cherries that have been soaking in kirsch for months. Sometimes I simply open a can of sour cherries, add kirsch, and let them sit for half an hour. Whichever version I use, it is always a big hit—after all, its base is a wonderful chocolate cake.

When making the genoise, the most important secret is to beat the eggs very well. (The eggs should be at room temperature, or they may be warmed by immersion in warm water for several minutes.) This allows the most amount of air to be incorporated into the cake. Sifting the flour (use a fine-mesh strainer) is a crucial step; it will make the flour incorporate easily with the eggs. The more you have to mix the batter, the more air you will lose from it.

Although baking powder is not traditionally included in a genoise recipe, I always add it to assure a perfect cake—and your guests will never know.

This cake freezes well if wrapped tightly in plastic wrap after cooling. If you have an inclination to whip up a fabulous dessert at the last moment, a frozen genoise might come in handy.

CHOCOLATE GENOISE:
> *5 whole eggs*
> *3 egg yolks*
> *1 cup sugar*
> *¼ teaspoon vanilla extract*
> *½ cup cake flour*
> *½ cup cocoa powder, preferably imported*
> *⅛ teaspoon baking powder*
> *2 ounces bittersweet chocolate, grated*

BASIC SYRUP:
> *2 cups water*
> *1 cup sugar*
> *1 lemon, unpeeled, cut into slices*
> *½ orange, unpeeled, cut into slices*

FILLING:

> *3 cups heavy cream*
> *3 tablespoons confectioners' sugar*
> *1 package unflavored gelatin dissolved in*
> *¹/₄ cup water (see directions on page 90)*
> *1 cup syrup, flavored with*
> *3 tablespoons kirsch*
> *3 cups pitted sour cherries, marinated overnight in*
> *¹/₄ cup sugar and*
> *3 tablespoons kirsch*

GARNISH:

> *1 small can pitted Bing cherries*
> *Chocolate curls or shavings*

To make the genoise: Preheat oven to 350° F.

Line the bottom of a 10-inch springform pan with parchment paper and butter the sides of the pan.

Beat the whole eggs, yolks, sugar, and vanilla extract with an electric mixer until the batter forms a ribbon or you can draw a ridge in it with your finger, about 10 to 15 minutes.

Sift together the flour, cocoa, and baking powder and fold into the batter, gently but thoroughly. Fold in the grated chocolate.

Pour the batter into the prepared pan and bake for about 40 minutes or until the cake springs back to the touch. Cool in the pan for 10 minutes, then unmold and cool on a cake rack.

To make the syrup: Combine all ingredients in a saucepan. Bring to a boil, stirring occasionally. Simmer for about 20 minutes.

Strain and cool. This can be kept for several weeks in a glass jar in the refrigerator.

To make the filling and assemble: Whip the heavy cream. As it starts to thicken, add the confectioners' sugar, then the dissolved gelatin, and continue whipping until the mixture is stiff.

Cut the genoise into 3 layers. Put the bottom layer of cake on a serving platter and brush it with some of the kirsch-flavored syrup.

Fit a pastry bag with a number-5 star tube. Fill with the whipped cream and pipe a ring around the outer edge of the layer and one in the center. Then pipe another ring between the two. Arrange sour cherries between the rings.

Top with the second layer, brush it with syrup, and follow the same procedure as above.

Place the last layer on top and spread top and sides with whipped cream. Make 16 rosettes around the top edge of the cake. Place a Bing cherry on each and sprinkle chocolate curls or shavings in the center of the cake.

CHOCOLATE CAKE

SERVES: 14 TO 16

THIS is a flourless chocolate cake, very light and airy. Serve it with Vanilla Custard Sauce (page 115), Raspberry Sauce (page 115), or Hot Chocolate Sauce (page 115). I also like it plain, with a dollop of whipped cream on the side.

½ pound bittersweet chocolate, cut into small pieces
⅓ cup light rum
1 teaspoon vanilla extract
8 eggs, separated
½ cup superfine sugar plus
½ cup superfine sugar

Preheat oven to 350° F.

Line the bottom of a 10-inch round cake pan with parchment paper and butter the sides.

Combine the chocolate with the light rum and vanilla extract and melt over very low heat in a heavy saucepan or double boiler. Let cool.

With an electric mixer, beat the egg yolks with ½ cup superfine sugar until light and fluffy. Fold the chocolate mixture into the egg yolk mixture.

In a separate bowl and using clean beaters, beat the egg whites. When they start to get frothy, add the remaining ½ cup sugar and continue beating until the whites are stiff. Fold the egg whites into the chocolate mixture, combining thoroughly but gently.

Pour the batter into the cake pan and bake for 25 minutes or until the cake springs back to the touch.

Cool the cake on a cake rack. Then put on a serving platter and serve plain or with your choice of sauce or whipped cream on the side.

ALBERT'S CHEESECAKE

SERVES: 14 TO 16

IT is my great privilege to have Albert Kumin as my friend. I consider him to be one of the finest pastry chefs in the world. To him, baking is like breathing—there isn't anything he does not know about it. He is also one of the kindest men in the world.

This cheesecake recipe is my favorite. It is neither too rich nor too light. Its texture is light rather than dense. As far as I am concerned, you cannot improve on this recipe—but that's my opinion. Try this and make up your own mind.

Here are some important hints:

• You may use a thin layer of baked sponge cake for the crust or make the Graham Cracker Crust given here.

• Stirring the top of the batter just before putting the cake in the oven will prevent the top from cracking.

• Check the cake after 40 minutes. If the top is getting too brown, cover it with a piece of parchment paper or buttered aluminum foil.

• After 1 hour, press the top of the cake with your finger. If the surface springs up again, the cake is done.

• This cake must be cooled slowly in the pan at room temperature. Put the pan on a cake rack so air will circulate under the bottom.

• When the cake is cooled, invert onto a plate and then invert again onto another plate, so it ends up right side up. If it is not to be served immediately, refrigerate it.

• This is a rich, creamy cake, so it is hard to cut with a knife. I suggest using a wire cake cutter, or simply take a piece of very strong thread, wrap it around the fingers of both hands, and press it down, cutting the cake in half, then in quarters, and so on.

GRAHAM CRACKER CRUST:
> 1½ cups graham cracker crumbs, about 20 cracker squares
> ⅓ cup butter, softened
> ½ cup sugar

CAKE:
> 2½ pounds cream cheese, at room temperature
> 1½ cups sugar
> 7 eggs
> 4 egg yolks
> 1 teaspoon vanilla extract (or grated rind of 1 lemon)
> ½ cup heavy cream

To make the crust: Blend all ingredients together.

To make the cake: Preheat oven to 400° F.

Cream the cream cheese with an electric mixer until very light and fluffy. Add the sugar, eggs, and egg yolks and cream well. Scrape down the sides of the bowl several times with a rubber spatula. Add the vanilla or lemon and beat well until the batter is smooth. Add the heavy cream and continue mixing.

Butter a deep 9-inch cake pan (not a springform pan) and cover the bottom with the graham cracker crust or a thin layer of baked sponge cake. Pour the batter into the cake pan.

Put the cake pan into a larger baking pan. Place it on the middle rack of the oven and pour boiling water into the larger pan until it reaches a level halfway up the cake pan.

Stir the top of the batter with a spoon. Bake for about 1 hour. Cool in the pan.

CHOCOLATE CHEESECAKE

SERVES: 20

IF you like chocolate and you like cheese, this is the perfect combination. I know that Billy Rose thought this was the greatest. I made it the very first time for his birthday dinner, and he flipped!

Try it the next time you are planning a birthday dinner for someone special in your life, and see if he doesn't agree with Billy Rose that this makes the best birthday cake ever.

NOTE: This is a very rich cake, so serve in small slices.

2 8½-ounce packages chocolate wafers
½ teaspoon cinnamon
½ cup (1 stick) butter, melted
16 ounces semisweet chocolate, cut into small pieces
1 cup sugar
4 eggs
1½ pounds cream cheese, softened
1 teaspoon vanilla extract
2 tablespoons cocoa
3 cups sour cream
¼ cup butter, melted

GARNISH:
Chocolate shavings (or candied violets and whipped cream)

Preheat oven to 350° F.

In a food processor or with a rolling pin, crush the chocolate wafers. You should have about 2 cups. Mix well with cinnamon and the ½ cup melted butter. Press the crumbs firmly to the bottom and sides of a 9-inch springform pan. Chill.

Melt the chocolate in a heavy saucepan over low heat or in a double boiler.

Beat the sugar with the eggs until light and fluffy. Add the cream cheese gradually, beating well after each addition. Add the melted chocolate to the egg mixture along with the vanilla, cocoa, and sour cream, beating constantly. Add the melted butter. Mix well.

Pour the mixture into the chilled cookie crust and bake for 45 minutes.

Remove cake from oven, cool it, and chill it overnight in the refrigerator.

To serve, remove from springform pan and decorate with chocolate shavings or candied violets and whipped cream.

RUM RAISIN RICE PUDDING

SERVES: 6

WHILE this is one of the "feel-good" recipes in my repertoire, it is definitely a rice pudding for grown-ups rather than children and, in my opinion, the best recipe for rice pudding. I sometimes serve it with Raspberry Sauce (page 115) on the side.

1 cup golden seedless raisins
1 cup dark rum, preferably Myers's
½ cup Carolina rice

2 cups water
Salt
1 quart milk
¹/₂ cup sugar
4 egg yolks
2 cups milk
1 tablespoon vanilla extract
1¹/₂ cups heavy cream, whipped with
¹/₄ cup confectioners' sugar

Soak the raisins in the dark rum for a few hours, preferably overnight.

Put the rice, water, and a little salt into a large saucepan, bring to a boil, and cook for 5 minutes. Drain, rinse with cold water, and return to saucepan. Add the quart of milk and the sugar and bring to a boil. Lower heat and simmer for about 45 minutes, uncovered, until most of the milk is absorbed.

In a bowl, beat the egg yolks lightly, add the milk, the vanilla extract, the raisins, and about 2 tablespoons of the rum that the raisins soaked in. Pour this into the rice and stir until the mixture has thickened. Do not let it boil.

Remove from heat and refrigerate.

When the pudding is thoroughly chilled, fold in the whipped cream and serve.

APPLE BREAD PUDDING (OFEN-SCHLUPFER)

SERVES: 6

THIS is one of the dishes my mother made when I was a child. The older I get, the more I realize how much I like it, and I find that a lot of other people feel the same way. It is another "feel-good" food.

The amount of ingredients can vary, depending on the size of your dish. Don't worry about exact amounts.

You may serve this with Vanilla Custard Sauce (page 115) on the side.

1 Italian or French bread, thinly sliced
3 apples, peeled, cored, and thinly sliced
1¹/₂ cups seedless raisins
³/₄ cup sugar
6 eggs
1 quart milk
1 teaspoon vanilla extract

Preheat oven to 350° F.

Butter an ovenproof dish. (I use my Pyrex lasagna pan.) Put a layer of sliced bread on the bottom, then a layer of the sliced apples. Sprinkle the apples with raisins and sugar. Continue layering until the dish is filled or you run out of ingredients, ending with a layer of bread sprinkled with some sugar.

Combine the eggs, milk, and vanilla extract in a blender or in a bowl with a whisk. Pour over the bread and apple mixture.

Bake for 1 hour. Serve while still warm.

ETCETERA

HERE are some useful odds and ends, including stocks and a variety of sauces.

5 pounds veal bones

3 pounds veal shanks or trimmings

1 carrot, coarsely chopped

2 stalks celery, coarsely chopped

1 onion, peeled and cut into quarters, one quarter stuck with a whole clove

1 whole leek, coarsely chopped

1 bouquet garni: 3 sprigs parsley, 1 bay leaf, and 1 celery leaf, tied together with cotton string

6 peppercorns

1 teaspoon salt

Cold water to cover the ingredients by 1 full inch

BROWN VEAL STOCK

YIELD: ABOUT 3 QUARTS

Brown the bones, meat, and vegetables in a little vegetable oil in a sauté pan on the stove or in a roasting pan in the oven at 450° F. for about 30 minutes, or until browned. (I prefer the sauté pan, since it goes faster and uses less energy.)

Put the browned ingredients into a large stockpot along with the remaining ingredients and bring to a boil. Remove the scum that rises to the surface. Reduce the heat to the lowest level and simmer the stock for approximately 5 hours.

Remove the meat and bones from the stock, strain it, and skim off the fat. If not for immediate use, cool the stock and put it into containers. Freeze it or store it in the refrigerator, where it will keep for at least one week.

For a more concentrated stock, simply return the strained stock to a clean saucepan and continue simmering it to reduce it to the strength you wish.

FISH STOCK

YIELD: ABOUT 2 QUARTS

THE eggshells in this recipe absorb the surface scum.

NOTE: Make sure not to use bones from strong-flavored fish such as bluefish and mackerel.

> *2 pounds fish bones, skin, and heads*
> *1 onion, stuck with a whole clove*
> *1 stalk celery, coarsely chopped*
> *1 carrot, coarsely chopped*
> *1 whole leek, coarsely chopped*
> *1 bouquet garni: 3 sprigs parsley, 1 bay leaf, and 1 celery leaf, tied together with cotton string*
> *3 cups dry white wine*
> *2 cups water*
> *6 peppercorns*
> *1 teaspoon salt*
> *Shells of 3 eggs*

Combine all ingredients in a large, heavy saucepan and bring to a boil. Lower heat and simmer for 40 minutes.

Strain.

SHRIMP STOCK

NEXT time your recipe calls for raw shrimp that you have to clean, take the shells and put them into a saucepan. Cover them with water and a little dry white wine and add some fresh parsley or dill. Bring to a boil and simmer for about 20 minutes, then strain and discard the shells.

This stock may be used in sauces that go with shrimp, or it can substitute for fish stock. If you have lobster shells, you may make them into stock in the same way.

CHICKEN STOCK

YIELD: ABOUT 2 QUARTS

WHENEVER I make chicken, I generally buy whole ones and cut them up myself, reserving the trimmings in the freezer until I have enough to make chicken stock.

6 pounds chicken backs, wings, skin, or other parts
1 carrot, coarsely chopped
2 celery stalks, coarsely chopped
1 onion, peeled and cut into quarters
1 whole leek, coarsely chopped
1 bouquet garni: 3 sprigs parsley, 1 bay leaf, and 1 celery leaf, tied together with cotton string
6 peppercorns
1 teaspoon salt
Cold water to cover the ingredients by 1 full inch

Put all the ingredients into a large stockpot and bring to a boil. Remove the scum that rises to the surface. Reduce the heat to its lowest point and simmer stock for approximately 3 hours.

Remove the meat and bones from the stock, strain it, and skim off the fat. If not for immediate use, cool the stock and put it into containers. It will last for at least one week in the refrigerator, or you may freeze it.

If you would like to have a more concentrated stock, simply return the strained stock to a clean saucepan and continue simmering it to reduce it to the strength you wish.

PÉRIGORDINE SAUCE

YIELD: 2½ CUPS

THIS is the classic accompaniment for fillet of beef and filet mignon.

Truffles are very expensive. When you open a can, put the unused ones in a glass jar and cover them with Madeira. Store in the refrigerator.

4 tablespoons butter
4 tablespoons flour
2¹/₂ cups condensed beef broth
1 teaspoon meat extract (Bovril)
¹/₂ cup Madeira wine
2 tablespoons finely chopped black truffles
Salt and pepper to taste

In a heavy saucepan, melt the butter. Stir in the flour over moderate heat. When the mixture begins to bubble, lower the heat and continue cooking for 8 to 10 minutes, stirring often, until the roux is a nut-brown color. Add the beef broth and stir with a wire whisk until the mixture begins to thicken and comes to a boil. Add the meat extract, Madeira, truffles, and seasoning and simmer for 2 minutes.

ROASTED RED PEPPER SAUCE

YIELD: ABOUT 3 CUPS

THIS sauce can be made up to a day ahead.

3 red bell peppers
4 large garlic cloves, unpeeled
5 tomatoes, peeled, seeded, and coarsely chopped
2 cups condensed chicken broth
1 tablespoon fresh oregano (or ½ tablespoon dried)
Salt and pepper to taste

Wash peppers and place over the flame of a gas burner or under a broiler, turning them often, until the skin is black.

Roast unpeeled garlic in a heatproof glass pan or baking sheet in a 400° F. oven for 20 minutes. Peel.

Peel the roasted peppers with a small paring knife, remove the seeds, and cut them into chunks. Put them into a medium saucepan along with the tomatoes, garlic, chicken broth, oregano, salt, and pepper. Bring to a boil and simmer for 15 minutes. Cool briefly.

Puree mixture in a blender.

Return mixture to the saucepan and reheat. Check for seasoning. If sauce is too thin, thicken it with a little cornstarch (about 1 teaspoon) mixed in cold water.

APRICOT SAUCE

YIELD: ABOUT 2 CUPS

THIS great dessert sauce may be served hot or cold.

1 pound dried apricots, covered with water and soaked overnight
¼ cup white wine

Combine apricots, the water in which they were soaked, and wine in a heavy saucepan. Bring to a boil and simmer for 15 minutes. Cool.

Put mixture in a blender and puree. If the sauce seems too thick, add a little water or apricot brandy.

YOU can substitute strawberries for the raspberries to make strawberry sauce.

> 2 cups fresh raspberries (or 1 10-ounce package frozen raspberries, thawed)
> ½ cup red currant jelly
> 1 tablespoon Framboise (raspberry brandy), optional

Put the raspberries, currant jelly, and Framboise, if using, in a blender and blend until well combined. Put this sauce through a strainer in order to remove the seeds.

RASPBERRY
SAUCE

YIELD: ABOUT 2 CUPS

> 2 eggs
> 2 egg yolks
> 1 cup sugar
> 1 tablespoon vanilla extract
> 2 cups hot milk

In the top of a double boiler, combine the whole eggs, yolks, sugar, and vanilla. Then add the hot milk and stir over simmering water until the sauce coats a spoon.
Remove from heat and serve.

VANILLA CUSTARD SAUCE

YIELD: 3 CUPS

THIS sauce is good on ice cream or on a hot soufflé. When cooled, it can be used as a frosting.

> 12 ounces semisweet chocolate
> ½ cup (1 stick) butter
> 1 cup sugar
> 1 teaspoon vanilla extract
> 1 cup heavy cream

Melt chocolate and butter in a heavy saucepan or in a double boiler over low heat. Add sugar, vanilla, and heavy cream. Simmer for 5 minutes or until smooth, stirring constantly.

HOT CHOCOLATE SAUCE

YIELD: 2 CUPS

CRÈME FRAÎCHE

YIELD: 1 CUP

THIS crème fraîche recipe will work only with heavy cream that has not been ultra-pasteurized. If it is not available, simply whip some heavy cream to light peaks and add the buttermilk, or mix 1 cup sour cream with ½ cup heavy cream and omit the buttermilk.

1 cup heavy cream, not ultrapasteurized
2 tablespoons buttermilk

Combine cream with buttermilk, mixing well. Cover lightly with plastic wrap. (Do not seal.)

Leave at room temperature for 12 to 24 hours, at which point it will have thickened. Then cover well and keep refrigerated until serving time. It will last for at least 5 days in the refrigerator.

MENUS

THE following chapter contains suggested menus for some special occasions. All of the recipes, of course, can be served separately or exchanged for others in this book.

I added this chapter because many people ask me what to serve when and how to put a menu together. Some basic rules can help you to create your own menus.

1) Avoid several heavy dishes in the same menu. For example, a cream-based soup before a main course with a cream sauce would be too much.

2) Think of the combination of colors and textures. Aim for complementary colors and textures as well as variety.

3) Try to use ingredients that are in season.

4) At formal meals around a table, think about whether the foods you choose can be comfortably eaten with a knife and fork. When you serve a buffet, where people have their plates on their laps, choose strictly fork food. If you give a formal-dress dinner, avoid hard-to-eat foods with bones (you don't want the food to end up in the lap of an expensive gown).

5) Think of the things you like to prepare. The results will be tastier.

6) Above all, don't worry too much: have a good time, and enjoy!

Crêpes Filled with Salmon, Crème Fraîche, and Caviar (page 120)

Fillet of Beef with Roasted Red Pepper (page 114) and Cornichon sauces (page 121)

118

Red and Yellow Pepper Mélange (page 122)

Raspberry Cheese Torte (page 123)

119

CRÊPES FILLED WITH SALMON, CRÈME FRAÎCHE, AND CAVIAR

SERVES: 8

THIS recipe is also good for Sunday brunch.

Crème fraîche is now commonly available, and it can also be made easily (page 116).

Choose caviar according to your budget. Fresh salmon caviar is quite nice and widely available. I often use three different-colored caviars atop the crêpes: red salmon, golden whitefish, and black beluga.

The crêpes should be made ahead of time, and all the ingredients, except for the caviar and the crème fraîche, should be at room temperature. I prefer to use an 8-inch Teflon, Silverstone, or other nonstick-finish pan to make the crêpes, since I find the traditional cast-iron crêpe skillets a pain to use and to clean.

¾ cup milk
¾ cup flour
2 eggs
1 tablespoon fresh dill
2 tablespoons butter, melted
About 1 tablespoon butter
1½ pounds smoked salmon, thinly sliced
1 cup crème fraîche (page 116) or sour cream
8 ounces caviar, red, yellow, black, or a combination
Fresh dill for garnish

Combine the milk, flour, eggs, and dill in a blender and blend well. Add melted butter and blend well again, scraping down the sides. Let sit for 30 minutes. (Gluten in the flour expands in the liquid. This should happen during the resting period rather than in the pan, or you will get pancakes instead of crêpes.)

In a crêpe pan or small skillet (see above), melt a little butter over medium heat. When the pan is very hot, wipe excess butter from it with a paper towel. Pour in enough batter to just cover the bottom of the pan. When crêpe is lightly browned around the edges, turn it quickly with a small metal spatula and cook it for another 2 seconds. Turn crêpe out onto a piece of waxed paper or aluminum foil, cover with another piece of paper or foil, and continue with the remaining batter.

Starting with the crêpes at room temperature, put a generous slice of smoked salmon on top of each crêpe. Fold crêpe in half or roll it, if you prefer. Put a generous spoonful of crème fraîche or sour cream on top. Garnish with a generous spoonful of caviar, or a bit of two or three colors of caviar. Top with a sprig of dill and serve.

FILLET OF BEEF WITH CORNICHON SAUCE

SERVES: 8

I F you start with a good cut of beef, all you have to do is roast it and serve it with a great sauce. This wonderful and unusual sauce is from *Gourmet* magazine, where I was chef of the executive dining room for three years. This was one of the favorite dishes there.

Two other sauces that can be served with the fillet are Périgordine Sauce (page 113) and Roasted Red Pepper Sauce (page 114).

Preheat oven to 400° F.

Trim the beef of all excess fat and tie the fillet with kitchen twine to hold its shape. (It will also cook more evenly when tied.) Season with salt and pepper.

Roast the fillet of beef for 30 minutes (to medium rare). Serve with the Cornichon Sauce.

CORNICHON SAUCE:
  2 cups white wine
  3 tablespoons shallots
  1 tablespoon dried tarragon (or 2 tablespoons fresh)
  1 cup (2 sticks) butter, softened
  2 tablespoons Dijon mustard (or 3 tablespoons whole-grain mustard)
  10 cornichons, julienned and halved
  ¼ cup heavy cream

Combine wine, shallots, and tarragon in a medium saucepan. Over medium heat, boil until the mixture is reduced by half.

With an electric mixer, beat together softened butter and mustard until fluffy.

Add mustard butter and cornichons to the reduced wine mixture. Heat sauce, making sure that the mixture does not come to a boil (otherwise the butter might separate).

Just before serving, stir in ¼ cup heavy cream.

RED AND YELLOW PEPPER MÉLANGE

SERVES: 8

THIS is a lovely, colorful vegetable dish. If you prefer not to roast the peppers, just cut them in strips without first removing the skins.

2 red peppers
2 yellow peppers
1 tablespoon virgin olive oil
1 tablespoon butter
Salt and pepper to taste
1 tablespoon chopped fresh parsley

Wash peppers and place over the flame of a gas burner or under a broiler, turning them often, until the skin is black.

Remove blackened skin with a small paring knife or under running water and cut peppers into uniform long strips.

Sauté peppers in the oil and butter and season with salt and pepper. Just before serving, sprinkle with chopped parsley.

DUCHESSE POTATOES

SERVES: 8

THIS is still one of the great classic potato dishes.

It can be made a few hours ahead of time, but it should not be refrigerated; the potatoes simply do not taste the same after refrigeration. Just warm them through when ready to serve.

6 medium-size cooking potatoes
1 teaspoon salt
Pepper to taste
1/4 teaspoon ground nutmeg
2 whole eggs
2 egg yolks
Half-and-half, if necessary

Peel potatoes and cut them into quarters. Steam them over water until soft, then put them through a potato ricer or food mill. Whip the potatoes with an electric mixer, then add the salt, pepper, and nutmeg.

Beat the whole eggs and yolks together until light and foamy. Add this to the potatoes. If they are too firm, add a little half-and-half. Whip until fluffy.

On a buttered cookie sheet, pipe out individual portions with a pastry tube in a spiral shape. This may be done a few hours earlier, but do not refrigerate; leave at room temperature.

Just before serving time, preheat oven to 350° F. Cover potatoes loosely with aluminum foil supported by toothpicks, so that the potato spirals do not get smashed. Bake about 10 minutes.

Remove aluminum foil and toothpicks. Raise oven temperature to 450° F. and bake until potatoes are lightly browned, which should take only a few minutes. (If left to cook longer, potatoes will dry out.)

THIS is my great all-purpose celebration cake. It originally started as a strawberry cheese torte, and it can also be made with fresh peaches, kiwi fruit, or pineapple. The combination of the light genoise and the rich frosting and filling with the slightly acidic fruit is wonderful.

Sometimes, for a unique presentation, I slice the cake into a pentagon shape. At times I have made it in three tiers for a wedding cake.

This cake should be made the day before serving. You might want to decorate it in the afternoon (see page 104 for directions on making the genoise).

When making the raspberry filling, or any other gelatin-based filling, you must be sure that the gelatin is completely dissolved before adding it to the fruit mixture. To do this, first soften the gelatin by sprinkling it over a small amount of liquid in a small glass heatproof dish. Let it sit for 2 minutes. After it is softened, place dish in a small pan of hot water. The gelatin is dissolved when the liquid looks clear.

SERVES: 12

GENOISE:
  5 whole eggs
  3 egg yolks
  1 cup sugar
  1/4 teaspoon vanilla extract
  3/4 cup all-purpose flour
  1/4 cup cornstarch
  1/8 teaspoon baking powder

RASPBERRY MOUSSE:
  2 cups pureed raspberries
  1 1/2 packages gelatin, dissolved in
  1/4 cup cold water (see above)
  1 cup heavy cream, whipped
  1/4 cup superfine sugar

CREAM CHEESE MIXTURE:
  1/2 pound cream cheese, at room temperature
  1/2 cup superfine sugar
  1/2 package unflavored gelatin, dissolved in
  1/4 cup water (see above)
  1 teaspoon vanilla extract
  1 1/2 cups heavy cream

RASPBERRY MIXTURE:
  2 pints raspberries
  2 tablespoons Framboise (raspberry brandy), optional

GARNISH:
  Fresh raspberries, about 16
  Mint leaves

MENUS

123

To make the genoise: Preheat oven to 350° F.

Line the bottom of a 10-inch springform pan with parchment paper and butter the sides of the pan.

In a large mixing bowl, add the eggs, egg yolks, sugar, and vanilla. Beat with an electric mixer until it is very light and fluffy and a spoonful of it forms a ribbon, about 10 to 15 minutes.

Combine the flour, cornstarch, and baking powder and sift it through a fine strainer. Add this mixture to the beaten eggs, folding it in thoroughly but very gently.

Pour the batter into the prepared pan and bake for about 40 minutes, until a toothpick inserted in the middle comes out clean or the cake springs back to the touch. Cool the cake on a rack for about 15 minutes, then remove it from the pan and continue cooling it on the rack.

When it is completely cool, cut the genoise into three layers.

To make the mousse: Add dissolved gelatin to raspberry puree. Mix well.

Whip heavy cream, adding the sugar as it thickens. When cream is whipped to stiff peaks, fold in the raspberry puree.

To make the cream cheese mixture: Mix the cream cheese with an electric mixer until smooth. Add the sugar and continue mixing until it is very light. Add the dissolved gelatin, then the vanilla extract.

Whip the heavy cream in an electric mixer until peaks form. Combine well by hand with the cream cheese mixture.

Reserve 1½ cups of this cheese mixture for frosting and decorating the outside of the torte.

To make the raspberry mixture: Sprinkle the Framboise over the raspberries and let them macerate for about 10 minutes.

To assemble: Put one layer of baked genoise in the bottom of a 10-inch springform pan. Pour the raspberry mousse mixture over this. Cover with another genoise layer. Pour the remaining cream cheese mixture over this layer. Cover the cream cheese layer with the macerated raspberries, then top with the third layer of genoise. Refrigerate the cake for at least 5 hours.

Invert cake on a serving platter so that the bottom becomes the top. Frost with the reserved cream cheese mixture and decorate with raspberries and mint leaves.

VALENTINE'S DAY DINNER

MENU
Black Mushroom Consommé
Marinated Lamb Chops
Wild Rice with Pine Nuts
Green Beans with Shallots
Coeur à la Crème

The idea behind this menu is *romance!* It is an easy-to-prepare menu, to give you time to relax; this is definitely one evening you want to enjoy as much as your guest(s). Who knows, if you handle things just right, you might just win your heart's desire.

BLACK MUSHROOM CONSOMMÉ

SERVES: 4 TO 6

I learned to make this wonderful soup when I worked for Jacqueline Kennedy. It is so easy to make that I am embarrassed when people ask me for the recipe—which, since it is one of the all-time great soups, happens all the time. It can be made the day before and reheated.

1 pound mushrooms, sliced
2 10½-ounce cans condensed beef broth
2 cans water
1 ounce (2 tablespoons) cognac
Salt and pepper to taste

Combine all ingredients in a saucepan and bring to a boil. Simmer for 40 minutes. Strain the mushrooms out and serve the consommé in cups.

A wealth of ripe berries, the components of delicious dessert sauces, sorbets, and tarts

MARINATED LAMB CHOPS

MARINATE the lamb the day before, cover and refrigerate, then leave it at room temperature for one hour before you cook it.

Use the same marinade for the lamb chops as you do for the Marinated Leg of Lamb (page 62) or omit the soy sauce and use lemon juice, garlic, and rosemary. This combination with lamb is like a marriage made in heaven.

NOTE: Be sure your oven is clean before you cook the lamb. Lamb needs a high temperature, and burn smells can spoil a romantic atmosphere. Put the lamb on a rack in a pan with water in the bottom. This prevents dripping fat from smoking when it hits the bottom of the pan.

Broil lamb chops (two per person) under a preheated broiler for approximately 5 minutes on each side, depending on the thickness. It will still be pink inside, which is how lamb tastes best.

WILD RICE WITH PINE NUTS

SERVES: 6 TO 8

I do not like to mix wild rice with regular rice, preferring to go all the way or not at all. (Actually, wild rice is not a rice but the grain of an aquatic grass.) When shopping, get ¼ pound of wild rice to serve two.

NOTE: Be careful not to overcook wild rice; it is best when it is a little crunchy.

1 cup wild rice
Cold water to cover rice
2 cans condensed chicken broth
2 tablespoons pine nuts
1 teaspoon vegetable oil

Put the wild rice into a saucepan with enough water to cover it. Bring to a boil and strain.

Return the rice to the saucepan and add the chicken broth. Bring to a boil and simmer, covered, for about 40 minutes or until all the liquid has been absorbed.

Sauté pine nuts in vegetable oil until lightly browned. Add just before serving.

GREEN BEANS WITH SHALLOTS

SERVES: 6 TO 8

PERFECT fresh green beans are the key to this recipe's success. They are perfectly cooked when still slightly crisp; it takes only about 5 minutes.

2 pounds green beans, washed and ends cut off
2 to 3 tablespoons vegetable oil
2 tablespoons finely chopped shallots
¼ cup water
½ to 1 teaspoon Spike Vegetable Seasoning

Cut green beans in half if they are long.

Heat vegetable oil in sauté pan. Add shallots and brown lightly. Add green beans. Stir until pan is hot again. Add ¼ cup water. Immediately cover pan. Leave heat on high for about 2 minutes, then turn off heat.

Let beans sit, covered, for 1 to 2 minutes to steam. Uncover and add Spike Seasoning just before serving.

COEUR À LA CRÈME

SERVES: 8

NEW food trends may come and go, but a great coeur à la crème is a classic and will always be in style. With a good recipe or a good dress, quality will endure.

This dessert is also very easy to make and can be prepared the day before. In fact, it is even better.

Fresh, good-quality ingredients are very important in this recipe. For the classic mixture, forget about substituting cottage cheese. It is a rich dessert, but one does not eat it every day. I prefer Philadelphia brand cream cheese here. Make sure the cream cheese is at room temperature and that the heavy cream is cold. (It whips more easily.)

If you cannot get fresh raspberries, use fresh strawberries. If you cannot get either, use frozen raspberries. Both fresh and frozen raspberries must be strained to remove the seeds. They get between the teeth—hardly the right note for a romantic dinner.

½ pound cream cheese
½ cup confectioners' sugar
Seeds of half a vanilla bean
2 cups heavy cream
Raspberry Sauce (page 115)
Several fresh berries for garnish

Beat the cream cheese with an electric mixer until light and fluffy. Add the confectioners' sugar and vanilla seeds and continue mixing until well combined.

If you have a heavy-duty mixer, simply add the heavy cream to the cream cheese mixture and continue beating until it is light and fluffy and forms soft peaks. Otherwise, whip the heavy cream separately until it forms soft peaks, then fold into the cream cheese mixture by hand with a rubber spatula.

Wring out a clean Handi Wipe or a large square of cheesecloth in cold water. Line a heart-shaped coeur à la crème mold with it. Fill well with the cream cheese mixture and carefully cover with the ends of the cheesecloth, then cover entirely with plastic wrap. Put mold on a pie plate to drain and place in the refrigerator for at least 6 hours, or overnight.

At serving time, remove the plastic wrap, turn back the ends of the cheesecloth, and unmold the Coeur à la Crème on a serving platter. Peel off the cheesecloth. Garnish with fresh berries, and serve with the Raspberry Sauce on the side.

This festive spring dinner offers Stuffed Leg of Lamb (page 132) flanked by Potatoes Provençale (page 133) and served with steamed asparagus, Carrots with Grapes (page 84), and Oeufs à la Neige (page 134) for dessert

Potatoes Provencale (page 133)

131

SPRING DINNER
MENU
Stuffed Leg of Lamb
Asparagus
Carrots with Grapes (page 84)
Potatoes Provençale
Oeufs à la Neige

Since spring is my favorite season, when so many of my favorite foods are fresh, I like to do a lot of entertaining then. I look forward to the first fresh asparagus in April, or to the wonderful fiddlehead ferns.

Although this menu may sound like a traditional Easter menu—and it can certainly be used for Easter dinner—it is really a great springtime dinner for any occasion. If you prefer to serve a ham for this type of dinner, see my recipe for Ham with Glaze and Mustard Sauce (page 65).

STUFFED LEG OF LAMB

SERVES: 8 TO 10

THIS is one of the classic French ways to prepare lamb. Although this recipe is in some of my other cookbooks, I did not want to omit it because it is my favorite way to prepare lamb. After years of making it, I still can't think of any improvements. The stuffing flavors the leg of lamb throughout; the lamb looks attractive when carved; and I love not having to fight with a bone when carving it.

1 leg of lamb, about 6 to 7 pounds, boned
Juice of 1 lemon
1/2 cup soy sauce
Salt and pepper to taste
2 tablespoons bread crumbs
1 clove garlic, put through a garlic press
1/2 cup finely chopped fresh parsley
1 teaspoon rosemary, crushed
1 carrot, coarsely chopped
1 onion, coarsely chopped
1 stalk celery, coarsely chopped
1/2 teaspoon rosemary, crushed
1 can condensed chicken broth
1 can condensed beef broth
1 cup dry white wine

Preheat oven to 400° F.

Lay the lamb, skin side down, on a flat surface and rub it with the lemon juice and soy sauce. Season it with salt and pepper.

Combine the bread crumbs, garlic, parsley, and rosemary and mix together well. Spread this mixture over the lamb and into the pockets left by the boning. Roll the meat into a cylindrical shape to enclose the stuffing completely. Tie it with string and put the lamb in a roasting pan.

Surround the lamb with the carrot, onion, celery, and ½ teaspoon rosemary and put it in the oven.

Mix the chicken broth, beef broth, and wine and baste the lamb with this liquid after 15 minutes of roasting. Continue basting every 10 minutes for another hour and 10 minutes.

Remove from oven and let the lamb rest for 10 minutes before carving. In the meantime, put the pan juices through a strainer to remove the vegetables. Reheat sauce before serving.

POTATOES PROVENÇALE

SERVES: 6 TO 8

THESE are the equivalent of German home fries. However, since home fries do not seem chic, we will call them Potatoes Provençale, since the thyme in the recipe is an herb from Provence.

The secret ingredient in these potatoes is goose fat. When I was a child, we always had a roast goose at Christmas. Its fat was saved from the roasting, so we had these potatoes only in the winter. Nowadays, goose fat is available year-round from such companies as Schaller and Weber, and it will keep for quite a while in the freezer. If you do not have goose fat, you can substitute bacon drippings.

Of course, these potatoes are terribly fattening, so don't get hooked on them!

24 medium new potatoes
1 pound sliced bacon, each slice cut into ¼-inch pieces
1 large onion, finely chopped
1 tablespoon thyme
2 tablespoons goose fat
Salt and pepper to taste
Fresh chives, snipped, for garnish

Peel or scrub and quarter potatoes. Steam them until they can be pierced with a knife but are still firm enough to offer a little resistance.

Preheat oven to 350° F.

In a large sauté pan, cook bacon until lightly browned. Add onion and thyme and sauté until onions are golden. Add goose fat and potatoes.

Transfer to roasting pan and roast in oven for 30 to 40 minutes, until they are brown. Season with salt and pepper and garnish with chives.

OEUFS À LA NEIGE

SERVES: 8

THERE is something about a custard dish that is comforting; it makes you feel like a kid being cared for. This is one of the ultimate fantasy custard dishes. Not only that, it is easy to make and very impressive!

The custard itself may be made up to a day ahead.

NOTE: Always poach meringues in water rather than milk, as the fat in milk will make them deflate. The water should be simmering, not boiling, otherwise they will disintegrate. I use an ice-cream scoop to make big, snowball-shaped meringues; tablespoons will create an egg shape. Don't put too many scoops in the water at once. They will expand due to the heat and crowd each other, and, afterward, they will slightly deflate. If you have difficulty turning the meringues, simply leave them to poach for a few minutes longer before trying again.

CAUTION: This is not the traditional way of making caramel, but it is my way. It is faster, but you must be very careful, since caramel is extremely hot. While making it, do not walk away; watch it carefully, as it can burn easily, and make sure that you have potholders handy.

The easiest way to clean the pan in which you make the caramel is to add water and put the pan back on the stove. Bring to a boil, and the caramel will dissolve.

CUSTARD:
>*2 cups milk*
>*1 cup heavy cream*
>*6 egg yolks*
>*2 whole eggs*
>*6 tablespoons sugar*
>*Dash of salt*
>*1 teaspoon vanilla extract*

MERINGUES:
>*6 egg whites*
>*Dash of salt*
>*¾ cup superfine sugar*
>*¼ cup confectioners' sugar*

CARAMEL:
>*1 cup sugar*

To make the custard: Heat milk and cream in the top of a double boiler until hot.

In the meantime, put the egg yolks, whole eggs, sugar, and salt into a mixing bowl and beat until light and fluffy. Add the warm milk and cream mixture to the egg mixture very slowly, stirring constantly.

Pour mixture back into the top of the double boiler and cook, stirring constantly, over hot, not boiling, water, until custard coats a metal spoon. Add vanilla extract.

Pour custard into serving dish and place in the refrigerator to chill.

To make the meringues: Fill a large sauté pan halfway with water and heat to simmering, or to 170° F.

Beat the egg whites with a dash of salt. When the egg whites are firm, add ¾ cup sugar and continue beating for 30 seconds. Then fold in ¼ cup confectioners' sugar by hand.

Using an ice-cream scoop or two tablespoons (see above), form the egg white mixture into large balls and drop them into simmering water. Poach them for 2 minutes on each side, then lift them onto a tray lined with paper towels.

To make the caramel: Melt 1 cup sugar in a heavy sauté pan on medium heat (see CAUTION). When the edges start to melt, stir occasionally. (If you stir too much, you get lumps. In this case, turn heat down to low and dissolve the lumps before turning up the heat again.) Continue cooking until sugar turns a light caramel color. Turn off the heat. If you are cooking on an electric stove, remove the pan from the heat source.

To assemble: Immediately before serving, place the meringues on the custard. Working carefully, dip a wooden spoon in the caramel and drizzle it in a stream over the meringues in a decorative fashion.

ENGLISH TEA

MENU
Watercress Sandwiches
Tomato Sandwiches
Smoked Salmon Sandwiches
Cucumber Sandwiches
Egg Salad Sandwiches

Scones with Raspberry Jam and Clotted Cream
Caramel-glazed Apple Tart
Lemon Sponge Cake
Pecan Nut Roll
Fudge Brownies
Strawberries Dipped in White and Dark Chocolate

Assorted Teas and Sherries

Other than Valentine's Day, I can't think of any occasion more romantic than an English tea. The combination of the food, the table settings, and the ambiance can transport you to a different time and place.

In New York, many fine hotels offer beautiful high teas. My favorite is the Stanhope, and I try to have tea there once a week or so; I love getting all dressed up for it and, while there, imagining myself in Victorian England.

Tea is a marvelous way of entertaining when lunch is too informal and dinner is too much. And, of course, a late afternoon tea in the middle of a long day provides a terrific break.

An English tea turned out to be the most appropriate theme for a bridal shower that I gave for my goddaughter, who happens to be the reincarnation of a Victorian romanticist. For this occasion, I hand-painted forty invitations. (Only love will inspire you to do things like this.) It was a smashing success. Many guests told me it was the best bridal shower they had attended, an unforgettable event.

While I was with Jacqueline Kennedy, I often prepared lovely teas for her guests.

We used many different assortments of savories and sweets. The varieties are endless, but some of the following basics are called for:

- Finger sandwiches, as necessary as the tea itself.
- Fresh, hot scones, with or without currants. In England, these are served with Devonshire cream, which is similar to crème fraîche.
- Raspberry jam, the very best you can buy.
- A pound cake or lemon cake, the basic sweet.

TEAS

SINCE there is such an interesting variety of teas available today, I thought I might list a few of my favorites and describe some of their flavors. Each and every one has a distinctive character.

Darjeeling: A light and evocative tea from a region of India bordering the Himalayas, this is my favorite tea in the summertime. There are many different varieties of Darjeeling. Some time ago I had the privilege to be invited to tea by the Indian ambassador, and he served me a vintage Darjeeling, which is in a whole different ballpark in terms of taste (and cost) from those we normally encounter. It was fabulous.

Earl Grey: A combination of China and Darjeeling, this is a good all-purpose tea to serve when you are not sure of your guests' preferences. It is a secret blend authenticated by the present Earl Grey. It is famed for its exceptional liqueur and delicate fragrance.

Lapsang Souchong: I drink this tea in the fall or when it is rainy because of its wonderful smoky flavor. This large-leaf tea comes from the Fukien province of China, where it grows in a very mineral-rich soil. It is slightly smoked, giving it a distinctive pungent flavor.

Russian Caravan: This comes from the Anwei province of China, and its blend of black China and brown Oolong teas makes for a heady brew. I favor Russian Caravan in the winter, and I add to it cream and Demerera sugar.

You ought to try all of them and pick your favorites. There are, of course, dozens of other varieties, ranging as widely in flavor as wines.

THE PROPER WAY TO MAKE TEA:

Start with fresh, cold water. Bring it to a boil, but do not let it boil for too long, or it will develop a flat taste. A whistling teapot is helpful, since it lets you know as soon as the water boils.

Preheat your china teapot by rinsing it with boiling water. Add tea leaves to the pot—one teaspoon per cup plus one "for the pot"—or put tea leaves into a tea egg or tea ball and place in the pot. Pour boiling water into the teapot and let tea steep for several minutes. Strain tea into another teapot or remove tea ball or tea egg before serving.

USE an assortment of breads and a variety of fillings. I have found that Pepperidge Farm's extra-thin-sliced bread works best. For an even look, cut the crusts off after filling the breads. Alternate the kinds of sandwiches on the serving tray, creating a profusion of different-colored centers.

Sandwiches may be made 1 to 2 hours in advance. Place a slightly damp paper towel over the sandwiches or cover with plastic wrap and refrigerate. If you don't have the time to make compound butters, use regular butter.

WATERCRESS SANDWICHES:
Put a stick of softened butter in the food processor. Add a few watercress leaves, washed and stems removed, 1 teaspoon lemon juice, and salt and pepper to taste. Process until smooth. If you don't have a food processor, simply chop the watercress finely and mix it with the other ingredients by hand.

Spread watercress butter on white or whole wheat bread, add some watercress leaves, top with a slice of bread, cut off crusts, and cut sandwich into triangles.

TOMATO SANDWICHES:
Spread thin-sliced white bread with plain butter. Add thinly sliced tomatoes and salt and pepper to taste. Top with buttered bread, cut off crusts, and cut into triangles.

SMOKED SALMON SANDWICHES:
Add horseradish to taste to softened butter. Spread on thin-sliced dark bread. Place thinly sliced smoked salmon on the bread and sprinkle over it lemon juice to taste. Top with bread, cut off crusts, and cut into triangles.

CUCUMBER SANDWICHES:
Spread thin slices of white bread with softened butter, then top with very thin slices of seedless cucumber. Sprinkle with salt and pepper and a little chopped dill. Cover with a second slice of buttered bread. Cut off crust on all sides, then cut sandwiches into triangles.

EGG SALAD SANDWICHES:
To 4 chopped hard-boiled eggs add ½ cup mayonnaise, 1 tablespoon Dijon mustard, salt, and pepper. Spread on thin-sliced white or whole wheat bread, top with bread, cut off the crusts, and cut sandwiches into triangles.

I learned about scones a long time ago, when I had a British boyfriend, who adored teas and food in general. As far as I'm concerned, being in love is the greatest inspiration to learning.

You can make the batter and shape it into scones up to two hours ahead of time. However, they should not be baked until just before serving time; they taste best when fresh and hot.

SANDWICHES

A lavish English tea may include such delicacies as Pecan Nut Roll (page 142), cookies, savory sandwiches, and scones

SCONES

YIELD: ABOUT 8 SCONES

2¼ cups flour
2 tablespoons double-acting baking powder
2 tablespoons sugar
½ teaspoon salt
4 tablespoons (½ stick) butter, cold, cut into pieces
3 eggs
½ cup light cream
¼ cup currants, optional

Preheat oven to 450° F.

Put the flour, baking powder, sugar, and salt into a food processor. Process for 20 seconds, then add the butter and process until well combined.

Mix the eggs and light cream together and add to the processor. Combine well. Finally, add the currants and process for another 2 seconds.

If you don't have a food processor, simply combine flour, baking powder, sugar, and salt in a large bowl and cut in the butter with a knife. Then add the egg and cream mixture, combine well, and mix in the currants.

Put the dough on a floured board and pat it out to a thickness of ¾ inch. Cut out rounds with a biscuit cutter and put them on a lightly buttered cookie sheet.

Bake for 15 minutes.

CARAMEL-GLAZED APPLE TART

SERVES: 6 TO 8

THE combination of caramel on the apples and the thin crust makes this one of the all-time great desserts. Since it is among the most popular desserts in my dining room, I make it frequently, using a jelly roll pan to yield numerous portions.

I find that Granny Smith apples work the best for this tart; they don't break and they have a nice acidity.

This tart may be made a day or two before serving. It keeps well covered in the refrigerator.

TART CRUST:
2 cups flour
¾ cup (1½ sticks) butter
¼ cup ground hazelnuts
⅓ cup ice water

FILLING:
4 Granny Smith apples, peeled, cored, and cut in half
1 cup sugar
½ cup apricot preserves

To make the crust: Combine flour, butter, and hazelnuts in a food processor and process until well combined. Add ice water and process until dough forms. (If you are not using a processor, see instructions for scones.)

Remove from processor, roll it out, and line a 9-inch tart pan with the dough or shape it into a rectangle on a cookie sheet.

Preheat oven to 350° F.

To make the filling: Take each apple half and cut into the thinnest possible slices of uniform size. Starting from the outside, arrange the slices in the tart shell in concentric circles. Place one slice on the next so that they almost completely overlap. You will have room for two large circles. Then arrange slices in an attractive pattern to fill the center.

Melt the sugar in a heavy saucepan over medium heat, stirring occasionally and keeping constant watch on it until it turns light caramel. Then quickly pour the caramel over the apples in concentric circles.

Place the tart on the middle rack of the oven and bake for about 35 minutes, or until the tart shell is nicely browned.

While the tart is cooking, melt the apricot preserves in a saucepan. Cool slightly. After the tart has come out of the oven but while it is still slightly warm, brush the top with apricot glaze.

Serve with whipped cream or crème fraîche (page 116).

LEMON SPONGE CAKE

SERVES: 16

THIS cake can be make up to a day ahead.

> *4 egg yolks*
> *2 whole eggs*
> *½ cup superfine sugar*
> *½ cup lemon juice*
> *1 tablespoon freshly grated lemon rind*
> *1¾ cups flour, sifted with*
> *¼ teaspoon salt*
> *4 egg whites*
> *1 cup superfine sugar*
> *Confectioners' sugar for garnish*

Preheat oven to 350° F.

With an electric mixer, beat the egg yolks and whole eggs with ½ cup superfine sugar until very thick and lemon-colored. On low speed, add the lemon juice and rind, then the flour. Combine well.

In another bowl, beat the egg whites with an electric mixer until they become foamy. With the mixer running, slowly add 1 cup superfine sugar and beat until the egg whites form stiff peaks.

Fold the lemon mixture into the egg white mixture by hand until they are well combined.

Pour the batter into an ungreased Gugelhopf or tube pan. Bake for 50 to 55 minutes or until the cake springs back when pressed with the fingers.

Invert the tube pan onto a bottle and let cake cool completely. Then remove from the bottle, loosen the cake lightly with a spatula, and invert onto a serving plate. Sprinkle with confectioners' sugar before serving.

PECAN NUT ROLL

SERVES: 12

Pecan Nut Roll

THIS dessert is one I often made for Billy Rose. While delicious, it is not terribly sweet, so it works well for a variety of occasions.

To give it an attractive presentation, I cut diagonal slices off each end before placing the roll on a serving tray. The cake may be made several hours ahead, filled before the guests arrive, and kept in the refrigerator. Wait until just before serving to sprinkle on the confectioners' sugar.

7 eggs, separated
½ cup confectioners' sugar, sifted
2 teaspoons vanilla extract
2 cups finely ground pecans
1 teaspoon baking powder
¼ cup confectioners' sugar, sifted
Confectioners' sugar for sprinkling
1 cup heavy cream
2 tablespoons confectioners' sugar
1 teaspoon vanilla extract
Confectioners' sugar for sprinkling

Preheat oven to 375° F.

With an electric mixer, beat egg yolks and ½ cup confectioners' sugar until the mixture is very thick and pale in color, about 10 to 15 minutes. Add the vanilla extract.

Mix the pecans with the baking powder and fold into the egg mixture.

In a separate bowl, beat the egg whites with an electric mixer until they begin to get stiff, then add ¼ cup confectioners' sugar and continue beating until stiff peaks form. Fold this into the egg yolk mixture, combining thoroughly but gently.

Line a 13-by-18-inch jelly roll pan with parchment paper. Spread the batter in the pan and bake for about 15 to 20 minutes, until a toothpick inserted in the center comes out clean. Remove the pan from the oven and let it cool for about 10 minutes.

While the cake is still warm, sprinkle the top of it with some confectioners' sugar. Cover the cake with a clean kitchen towel and turn the pan over to remove the pecan nut roll from the pan. Working from the long side, carefully peel off the parchment paper. Immediately roll cake up from the long side in the towel. Set aside until cool.

Combine heavy cream, 2 tablespoons confectioners' sugar, and vanilla extract and beat with an electric mixer until stiff peaks form.

Unroll the cake and spread it evenly with the whipped cream mixture. Roll the cake up again.

Just before serving, sprinkle with confectioners' sugar.

AT the time I went to work for Jacqueline Kennedy, John, Jr., was five years old. He loved these brownies and even helped me make them. I knew back then that he was one of the special people in this world, and I would like to dedicate this recipe to him. Anytime he wants some out of my freezer, all he has to do is call.

NOTE: The brownies will be very fudgy inside and not dry. They keep very well in the freezer.

9 ounces unsweetened chocolate
1 cup and 2 tablespoons (2¼ sticks) butter
9 eggs
4½ cups sugar
1½ tablespoons vanilla extract
2¼ cups flour
1½ cups chopped pecans

Preheat oven to 325° F.

In a heavy saucepan or double boiler, melt the chocolate with the butter over low heat, stirring occasionally. When the chocolate is melted, set aside to cool.

In a large mixing bowl, combine eggs, sugar, and vanilla extract and beat until light and fluffy. Add the cooled chocolate mixture. Combine well. Fold in the flour and pecans.

Line a 13-by-18-inch jelly roll pan with parchment paper, rubbing both the pan as well as the paper with a little vegetable oil. Pour the brownie batter into the prepared pan and bake for 25 minutes.

When cooled, cut into squares.

THIS is an elegant confection that looks lovely on a tea tray or cake stand nestled among your other pastries and sweets.

Many fine supermarkets now carry extra-large strawberries with long stems still attached. They cost more than the regular strawberries, but given the effect they create, they're worth it.

Grapes, orange slices, and pineapple are other candidates for dipping.

STRAWBERRIES DIPPED IN WHITE AND DARK CHOCOLATE

Clean large strawberries, leaving the stems intact, by brushing them off lightly with a paper towel.

Line a cookie sheet with aluminum foil.

Melt bittersweet chocolate over low heat in a double boiler. When the chocolate is melted, dip half the strawberries halfway down into the melted chocolate. Let excess drip off and put strawberries on the cookie sheet to cool.

Proceed in the same manner with the rest of the berries and the white chocolate.

I believe there are certain occasions whose symbols and traditions demand respect. One of these is Thanksgiving, when I wouldn't dream of serving anything but the traditional turkey dinner. This is also a time to forget about dieting and simply enjoy.

For this holiday, I love to bring the reds, golds, and oranges of the season into my home, so I decorate with autumn leaves, chrysanthemums, pumpkins, gourds, and, for good measure, miniature scarecrows.

APPLE CIDER PUNCH

SERVES: 8

I have two versions, one with Calvados (French apple brandy), one without:

1) Combine 2 quarts apple cider and 1 cup Calvados in a saucepan. Heat gently and serve in heatproof glasses with cinnamon sticks.

2) Warm 2 quarts of apple cider, add a pinch of cinnamon, and serve in heatproof glasses with cinnamon sticks.

E VERY time I serve this soup, people comment about the combination; it is truly one of the most popular soups in my dining room.

This recipe can be made in large batches, well ahead of time, and frozen.

1 small butternut squash (about 1 pound)

3 tart green apples, peeled, cored, and coarsely chopped

1 medium onion, coarsely chopped

¼ teaspoon rosemary

¼ teaspoon marjoram

3 cans condensed chicken broth

2 cans water

2 slices white bread

Salt and pepper to taste

¼ cup heavy cream

1 tablespoon chopped fresh parsley for garnish

Cut the butternut squash in half. Peel and seed it and cut it into chunks. Combine with the apples, onion, herbs, chicken broth, water, bread, salt, and pepper in a large heavy saucepan. Bring to a boil and simmer, uncovered, for 45 minutes.

Puree the soup in a blender, 2 cups at a time, until smooth. Return the soup to the saucepan and bring to a boil, then reduce the heat.

Just before serving, add the heavy cream. Serve hot with a sprinkle of parsley on top.

BUTTERNUT SQUASH AND APPLE SOUP

SERVES: 8

Thanksgiving must include turkey (page 148), of course, but the accompaniments make all the difference. Clockwise, from bottom: Butternut Squash and Apple Soup (page 145), Green Beans with Shallots (page 128), Sweet Potatoes with Maple Sugar and Apples (page 150), Apple Cider Punch (page 144), Cranberry Sauce, and Pecan and Pumpkin Tart (page 150)

147

TURKEY WITH SAUSAGE AND CHESTNUT STUFFING

SERVES: 8 TO 10

I generally try to get small turkeys, usually about 9 pounds, since they are more tender and juicier than larger birds. They also take less time to cook, so you don't have to get up at the crack of dawn to get the turkey on. If you are serving a large group, you might want to prepare two small turkeys, perhaps with two different kinds of stuffing.

Before roasting the turkey, I always put pats of butter between the skin and the breast meat. This works better than putting a slice of salt pork on top or brushing with butter or oil (which simply runs off). The butter under the skin stays there and keeps the breast meat juicy.

> *1 turkey, approximately 9 pounds*
> *Salt and pepper*
> *4 tablespoons butter*

STUFFING:
> *1 tablespoon butter*
> *1/2 cup finely chopped shallots*
> *1/2 pound sausage meat*
> *2 tablespoons butter*
> *Turkey livers, finely chopped*
> *1 cup croutons*
> *1/2 teaspoon thyme*
> *3 tablespoons finely chopped celery*
> *3 tablespoons finely chopped fresh parsley*
> *1 teaspoon salt*
> *1/4 teaspoon pepper*
> *1 cup whole canned chestnuts*
> *1 apple, peeled, cored, and finely chopped*
> *1/4 cup heavy cream*

FOR ROASTING:
> *2 onions, thickly sliced*
> *2 carrots, thickly sliced*
> *2 stalks celery, thickly sliced*
> *1/2 teaspoon thyme*
> *2 cups condensed chicken broth*

FOR GRAVY:
> *1 tablespoon butter, at room temperature, mixed with*
> *1 tablespoon flour*

Preheat oven to 325° F.

Season the turkey with salt and pepper. Starting from the back of the turkey, put pats of butter between the skin and the breast meat by easing your hand under the skin to loosen it away from the breast. Put about two pats of butter under the skin of each side of the breast.

To make the stuffing: Melt 1 tablespoon butter in a heavy skillet and add the shallots. Sauté until they are lightly browned. Add the sausage meat, breaking it up with a fork and cooking until it is lightly browned.

Transfer entire contents of the pan to a fine sieve, set over a small bowl, and let all the excess fat drain off.

In the same skillet, melt 2 tablespoons butter and add the turkey livers. Brown quickly, while turning constantly. Stir in the drained sausage meat mixture, croutons, thyme, celery, parsley, salt, and pepper. Mix well, then crumble the chestnuts and add them along with the apple and the heavy cream.

To roast the turkey: Fill the turkey loosely with the stuffing. Sew up the opening and truss the turkey securely. Place the turkey in a shallow roasting pan. Scatter the onions, carrots, celery, and thyme around the turkey, pour in the chicken broth, and put in the oven.

Roast the turkey for approximately 3 to 3½ hours, basting every 15 minutes with the chicken broth.

When the turkey is ready for serving, put it on a preheated platter and garnish with fresh parsley or to your fancy. Remove the thread that secured the opening and loosen some of the stuffing, so that it appears to be pouring out. Set aside and keep warm.

To make the gravy: Thin the butter and flour mixture with a little chicken broth. Add to roasting pan and place pan on top of stove. Bring to a boil, stirring constantly. Strain into a sauceboat and serve with the turkey.

SWEET POTATOES WITH MAPLE SUGAR AND APPLES

SERVES: 8 TO 10

I love sweet potatoes, and they taste even better combined with apples and maple sugar. Of course, they also add up to a lot of calories, but Thanksgiving only comes once a year.

If you want to save time, you may use canned sweet potatoes. Who is going to tell your guests? Not me.

This dish can be made several hours ahead and reheated.

½ cup (1 stick) butter
¾ cup maple sugar (or maple syrup)
3 Granny Smith apples, peeled, cored, and sliced
6 cooked sweet potatoes, peeled and cut into cubes
Milk

Preheat oven to 350° F.

In a sauté pan, melt the butter. Add the maple sugar or syrup and the apples. Stir to combine well. Cover and continue cooking until the apples are tender, about 4 minutes. Add the sweet potatoes and combine well.

When well mixed, transfer to a food processor and puree for a few seconds, adding a little milk if necessary. (Don't worry if it isn't totally smooth; personally, I like it a little chunky.)

Transfer the mixture to a well-buttered ovenproof dish. Sprinkle with a little more maple sugar or brown sugar and a few dots of butter, if you wish, and bake for about 20 minutes.

PECAN AND PUMPKIN TART

SERVES: 8 TO 10

THIS offers something a little different from the classic pumpkin pie without venturing too far from tradition. It can be made up to a day ahead.

TART CRUST:
    2 cups flour
    ½ cup (1 stick) butter
    3 tablespoons shortening, preferably Crisco
    ¼ cup pecans
    ⅓ cup ice water

FILLING:
    4 eggs, separated
    1 cup maple sugar (or packed light brown sugar)
    ½ teaspoon cinnamon
    ½ teaspoon nutmeg
    1 teaspoon vanilla extract
    2 cups pumpkin puree, canned or fresh

1 cup heavy cream
1/2 cup chopped pecans

To make the crust: In a food processor combine flour, butter, shortening, and nuts and process until it has the texture of cornmeal. Add the ice water, processing until the dough comes off the sides of the food processor. (If you are not using a food processor, see directions on page 140).

Roll out dough and line a 10-inch tart pan with this crust. Refrigerate it for 30 minutes.

Preheat oven to 450° F.

To make the filling: Beat egg yolks and sugar with an electric mixer until thick. With mixer at low speed, add the cinnamon, nutmeg, vanilla extract, pumpkin puree, heavy cream, and nuts, combining all ingredients well.

In another bowl, with clean beaters, beat the egg whites until stiff but not dry. Fold them gently into the pumpkin mixture, combining well.

Pour mixture into chilled pie crust and bake for 15 minutes. Reduce heat to 350° F. and continue baking for another 30 to 40 minutes, or until a knife inserted in the tart comes out clean.

Cool and refrigerate until serving time.

MAPLE ICE CREAM

SERVES: 10

I love the taste of maple sugar so much that I enjoy it on my cereal in the morning. It used to be that only maple syrup was available in the supermarket, but now I find granulated maple sugar in many places.

You may use either maple sugar or maple syrup for this recipe, but it should be *pure* maple syrup, not imitations. If you use syrup you don't need to heat the milk; the purpose of that step is to dissolve the sugar.

1 quart milk
3 cups maple sugar or syrup
2 quarts heavy cream

If using maple sugar, heat it together with the milk until the sugar dissolves. Cool. Otherwise, combine the milk and the maple syrup. Add the heavy cream. Combine thoroughly, put in an ice-cream maker, and follow the manufacturer's directions.

Serve on the side with Pecan and Pumpkin Tart or pumpkin pie.

CHRISTMAS DINNER

MENU
Oxtail Consommé
Oysters in Champagne Sauce
Pear Sorbet (page 101)
Saddle of Venison with Cassis Sauce
Spaetzle
Brussels Sprouts with Chestnuts
Red Cabbage
Lingonberries
Green Salad with Stilton Cheese (page 46)
Christmas Trifle

When I'm entertaining at Christmas, I feel that the way my home looks is more important than at any other time of the year. This is when I go all out with greens, flowers, candles, and decorations, so that as soon as my guests walk through the door, they feel the festive spirit of Christmas.

I decorate with an abundance of pine branches, white flowers, such as paper-white narcissi or carnations, and several pots of single amaryllis bulbs for a dramatic effect. I scatter dozens of small votive candles around the room. (Votives are easier to use and less dangerous than tapers.) A hint: scented candles interfere with the wonderful aromas and tastes of the food you are serving.

My Christmas party is always a black-tie dinner. Formal attire makes people feel special and immediately puts them in a festive mood. When my guests enter, I hand them a Kir Royale or a spicy wine punch, and we toast the joys of the season.

THIS soup has so much natural gelatin from the bones that it makes your lips stick together—a sign of a really good soup! It takes a little effort to make, but it is definitely worth the trouble, and it is one of those dishes that should be made properly or not at all. However, it can be made ahead and frozen.

OXTAIL CONSOMMÉ

SERVES: 10 TO 12

2 pounds oxtails, cut into 1-inch pieces (available in most supermarkets)
1 carrot, coarsely chopped
1 stalk celery, coarsely chopped
1 onion, cut into quarters
1 bay leaf
2 sprigs parsley
4 cans condensed beef broth plus
4 cans cold water
2 cups red wine
6 peppercorns
½ teaspoon salt
Chopped fresh parsley for garnish

Preheat oven to 450° F.

Place oxtails, carrot, celery, and onion in a roasting pan. Bake in the oven for about 30 minutes, or until brown. (You may brown the oxtails and vegetables in a little vegetable oil in a sauté pan instead. This is faster, but it needs tending.)

Put oxtails and vegetables in a stockpot and add remaining ingredients except for the chopped parsley. Bring to a boil. Simmer for 4 hours.

Strain soup and discard vegetables (unless you would like to save them for nibbling later). When soup is cool, refrigerate it, so that the fat can rise to the top and solidify, making it easy to remove all the fat from the soup.

At serving time, reheat soup and check for seasoning. Serve garnished with a sprinkling of parsley.

Among the goodies at a fabulous Christmas feast, clockwise from bottom left: Green Salad with Stilton Cheese (page 46), Christmas Trifle (page 159), Brussels Sprouts with Chestnuts (page 158), Red Cabbage (page 159), Saddle of Venison with Cassis Sauce (page 156) and Spaetzle (page 158), and Oysters in Champagne Sauce (page 156)

Served with strawberries and whipped cream, Vanilla Bavarian Cream (page 160) makes a dessert in itself

OYSTERS IN CHAMPAGNE SAUCE

SERVES: 6

THE most important thing to remember about preparing this recipe is that the oysters must be *very* fresh. My favorite are belon oysters, but any farm-raised variety will do. Order them to be delivered or picked up on the afternoon of your dinner party, and ask your fish man to open them for you. Mine sends them to me opened on a bed of crushed ice, so that they do not tip over.

Ask your fish man to reserve the juice from the shelling. Then strain it to eliminate any sand or shell chips.

5 pounds rock salt
24 fresh oysters, shucked and on the half shell
4 tablespoons butter
2 tablespoons finely chopped shallots
1 tablespoon flour
1 1/2 cups champagne
1/2 cup reserved oyster juice (or 1/2 cup champagne)
Salt and pepper to taste
1/2 teaspoon dry mustard, preferably Colman's
1/2 cup heavy cream
Chopped fresh parsley for garnish

Fill a jelly roll pan with rock salt. Place oysters on the half shell on top of the bed of salt.

Melt the butter. Add shallots and cook on low heat for a few minutes without letting them brown. Add flour, combine well, and cook for another minute. Add champagne and oyster juice. Simmer sauce for 10 minutes. Season it with salt, pepper, and dry mustard, combining well with a whisk. Whisk in the heavy cream.

Pour a little sauce over each oyster. Put under a preheated broiler for about 3 minutes (or longer, if your broiler is not very hot), just enough to warm them through. The edges of the oysters should be a little curled. Garnish with parsley.

SADDLE OF VENISON WITH CASSIS SAUCE

SERVES: 10 TO 12

THIS is strictly a fall and winter dish. Venison is now farm-raised in New York State. It is of excellent quality, having a less gamy flavor than the wild venison. I get mine from the Lucky Star Ranch Corp. in Chaumont, New York, which offers venison with a truly exceptional flavor.

I always have my saddles boned and the bones cut up to make venison stock for my sauce. The venison stock is an essential part of the Cassis Sauce, adding significantly to its flavor. It should be made the day before and refrigerated overnight in order to get rid of the fat.

NOTE: If you tie up the saddle with butcher string, it will retain its shape and cook more evenly.

VENISON STOCK:
Venison bones from the saddle of venison
1/2 carrot, cut into 1-inch pieces
1/2 onion, cut into quarters

1 stalk celery, cut into 1-inch pieces
3 quarts water
3 cups red wine
½ bay leaf
Salt and a few peppercorns

VENISON:
   3 tablespoons butter
   2 tablespoons vegetable oil
   1 saddle of venison, boned, about 6 pounds

CASSIS SAUCE:
   3 tablespoons shallots
   1 tablespoon flour
   4 cups venison stock
   ¼ cup good-quality cassis liqueur (or cassis puree)
   Salt and pepper, if necessary
   Cornstarch mixed with water, optional

To make the venison stock: Preheat oven to 450° F.

Roast bones, carrot, onion, and celery in a jelly roll pan in the oven for 20 to 30 minutes, or until lightly browned.

Place browned bones and vegetables in a large saucepan or stockpot and cover with the water and red wine. If it does not come to a level 2 inches above the bones, add more water. Add bay leaf, a few peppercorns, and a dash of salt. Bring to a boil. Simmer stock for several hours.

Cool, strain, and refrigerate, preferably overnight, long enough to give the fat a chance to rise to the surface. After this happens, get rid of as much of the congealed fat as possible.

To roast the venison: Preheat oven to 375° F.

Melt the butter and oil in a large sauté pan. If the saddle is too large to fit in one pan, cut it in half. Add the venison and, on medium-high heat, brown it well on all sides, taking care not to burn the butter. Set aside sauté pan to use for the Cassis Sauce.

Put the saddle in a roasting pan and roast it in the oven for 20 minutes. Venison, like fillet of beef, is best served medium to rare. If it is overcooked, it gets tough.

Slice and serve with Cassis Sauce.

To make the Cassis Sauce: To the same pan in which you browned the venison, add the shallots. Brown lightly for a few minutes without letting them get too dark. Add flour and venison stock and simmer for about 20 minutes. Add the cassis. Taste and add salt and pepper if necessary.

If you like, you may thicken this sauce a little with a cornstarch slurry (a little cornstarch mixed with some water). Use only enough to make it thick enough to coat a spoon. After thickening, put sauce through a strainer to get rid of any lumps.

SPAETZLE

SERVES: 6 TO 8

S PAETZLE is the first thing I remember making as a child in Germany. It is to Germans what pasta is to the Italians.

The traditional way of making these noodles is to spread the dough on a small wooden board and to cut them with a knife. Luckily, since my mother had a spaetzle machine, I never had to learn how to do that. Neither will you, because spaetzle machines are inexpensive and are now available at many gourmet shops and any good German grocery store.

Spaetzle can be make a few hours ahead, covered with aluminum foil, and reheated.

> 3 cups flour
> ³⁄₄ teaspoon salt
> 5 eggs
> ¹⁄₄ cup water

Put a large pot full of water on to boil and add a dash of salt. Mix the flour and salt in a bowl and make a depression in the center of it. Break the eggs into the depression. Beat the batter until it is smooth while adding the water. This mixture should be rather heavy and thick; if it is too thin, the spaetzle will be mushy. Work the dough well.

Put dough into the spaetzle machine and push it through into the pot of boiling water. When the spaetzle swim to the top and the water has returned to the boil—which takes only a few minutes—lift them out with a slotted spoon and put them into another pot filled with hot water. Repeat this process until all the dough is used.

Drain and serve.

BRUSSELS SPROUTS WITH CHESTNUTS

SERVES: 12

N OW that chestnuts come in jars from France already peeled and cooked, this recipe is a snap, But, of course, if you want to use fresh ones, go for it.

NOTE: Whenever you steam whole Brussels sprouts, cut a cross into the stem. This will allow them to cook faster and more evenly.

> 6 tablespoons butter
> 4 tablespoons maple sugar (or maple syrup)
> 1 1-pound jar chestnuts
> 3 pounds Brussels sprouts, steamed

Melt the butter in a heavy sauté pan. Add the maple sugar or syrup, then add the chestnuts and sauté them until they are glazed. Finally, add the Brussels sprouts, combine well, and heat them through.

RED CABBAGE

SERVES: 12

TO me, Christmas without red cabbage almost isn't Christmas. It is very traditional in my family.

I find the taste of cooked red cabbage even better the next day, so if you can make it the day before, do so. When you store it overnight, however, make sure to put it in an airtight, nonaluminum container, or it will change color.

3 medium heads red cabbage
2 tablespoons bacon drippings
1 medium onion, finely chopped
2 carrots, finely chopped
1½ cups condensed beef broth
1½ cups red wine
1 bay leaf
2 apples, peeled, cored, and finely chopped
2 tablespoons wine vinegar
Salt and pepper to taste

Remove the outer leaves and core of each cabbage. Cut them into quarters and then into medium-fine slices, as for coleslaw, or slice in your food processor.

In a large saucepan, heat the bacon drippings. Add the onion and carrots and sauté for approximately 3 minutes. Add the cabbage and toss well to coat it lightly with the bacon fat. Mix in beef broth, wine, bay leaf, apples, vinegar, salt, and pepper. Stir well and bring to a boil.

Reduce heat, cover, and simmer for 1 to 1½ hours, or until it achieves the consistency you prefer.

CHRISTMAS TRIFLE

SERVES: 12

THIS is undoubtedly one of the most involved recipes in my book, even more so than the recipe for Chocolate Normandy, but since it is for Christmas, I feel it is worth the special effort.

Ladyfingers may be used instead of the jelly roll, but it will not give the same result.

When making the raspberry filling, gelatin is added to thawed frozen raspberries. These should be at room temperature; if they are too cold, they will cause the gelatin to lump. See page 123 for further directions on dissolving gelatin.

To avoid big problems when you cook custards such as the Vanilla Bavarian Cream, keep a bowl filled with ice water next to the stove. If the custard looks as if it is about to boil—which will cause it to curdle—plunge the saucepan into the ice water to stop the cooking. By taking this precaution, you can make your custards in a saucepan rather than a double boiler, which takes twice as long. For this purpose, you need a good heavy saucepan; do not use one made of aluminum or cast iron, as either will change the color of the custard.

The trifle may be made the day before serving it. Note in the instructions for assembling the dessert (page 161) that the jelly roll and the raspberry filling need to be refrigerated for a while, during which time you can be making the Vanilla Bavarian Cream.

JELLY ROLL:

> *6 eggs, separated*
> *4 tablespoons sugar*
> *6 tablespoons sifted flour*
> *1 teaspoon vanilla extract*
> *Confectioners' sugar for sprinkling*
> *$^1/_2$ cup seedless red raspberry jam*

RASPBERRY FILLING:

> *1 package unflavored gelatin, dissolved in*
> *$^1/_4$ cup Framboise (raspberry brandy) or $^1/_4$ cup cold water*
> *2 10-ounce packages frozen raspberries in syrup, thawed and at room*
> *temperature*

VANILLA BAVARIAN CREAM:

> *2 cups milk*
> *6 egg yolks*
> *Seeds from $^1/_2$ vanilla bean (or 1 teaspoon vanilla extract)*
> *$^3/_4$ cup sugar*
> *$1^1/_2$ packages gelatin softened in*
> *$^1/_4$ cup cold water*
> *1 cup heavy cream, whipped*

TO ASSEMBLE TRIFLE:

> *About $^1/_2$ cup sweet sherry*
> *Whipped cream*
> *Raspberries*

To make the jelly roll: Preheat oven to 400° F.

Brush a 10-by-15-inch jelly roll pan with vegetable oil. Line it with parchment paper, allowing 2 inches overlap at either end, and oil the paper.

Beat the egg yolks and sugar with an electric mixer until the mixture is pale in color and thick enough to form a ribbon, about 10 to 15 minutes. Carefully fold in the sifted flour and the vanilla extract.

Beat the egg whites until stiff and fold them in gently.

Spread the batter in the prepared pan. Bake for about 12 minutes, or until it is golden brown and tests clean when a small skewer or toothpick is inserted. Let cool 5 minutes.

While cake is still warm, sprinkle it with confectioners' sugar and overturn it on a board covered with two long, overlapping sheets of waxed paper. Lift the pan off the cake and gently strip off the waxed paper from the bottom of the cake.

Spread the cake with the raspberry jam and carefully roll the cake up from the long side.

To make the raspberry filling: Sprinkle gelatin over Framboise or water in a small heat-proof cup. Mix well and let sit for 2 minutes. Place cup in a pan of hot water until gelatin is dissolved (when the liquid looks clear).

Add dissolved gelatin to thawed raspberries and syrup (see above). Combine well. Chill slightly.

To make the Vanilla Bavarian Cream: In a heavy saucepan (see above), scald the milk (heat it over low heat until just before it boils).

Beat egg yolks, vanilla, and sugar until creamy. Pour the heated milk gradually into the egg mixture, stirring constantly.

Cook mixture in a heavy saucepan or in a double boiler over simmering water, stirring constantly, until it coats the back of a spoon.

Remove from heat and add softened gelatin. Stir until dissolved.

Pour custard into a bowl and cool in the refrigerator until it just starts to thicken, or stand the bowl in another bowl filled with ice cubes and cold water. This will speed up the process. Stir custard occasionally with a whisk to cool it evenly.

Fold in the whipped cream.

To assemble: Cut jelly roll into ½-inch slices. Line bottom and sides of a 3-quart glass bowl with the slices in a decorative fashion. Sprinkle sweet sherry (no more than ½ cup) over the slices. Pour slightly chilled raspberry filling over the cake. Refrigerate until it is almost set.

Pour Vanilla Bavarian Cream over the raspberry filling. Chill until set.

Decorate with whipped cream rosettes and raspberries.

BREAKFAST

THE only meal that I do not enjoy cooking is breakfast. I have no idea why I feel that way, but that's the way it is. I happen to be fortunate enough today to have a wonderful chef who makes my breakfast for me every morning.

Having been the server of many breakfasts for the rich and famous, I know what breakfast in bed should be about, and I have it that way every morning. This is truly one of the greatest advantages of being in my business.

I am writing this because I feel it is important to spoil oneself at least every now and then. I realize that few are as fortunate as I am to have a chef to prepare breakfast, but you can still pamper yourself with breakfast on a tray or, better, persuade someone else to make it for you occasionally. I used to perform this service frequently for my daughter when she was small so that when she got older, she would know how to do it for me. It has not quite worked out that way, although Beatrice does make me fresh muffins and wonderful breakfast breads. In fact, her birthday present to me this year was a "bread of the month." Each month she bakes two different kinds of bread or muffins for me. Believe me, I take full advantage of this service.

A recent big trend in New York is the "power breakfast," where executives meet and make corporate decisions. On one of my television shows, John Mariani was doing a segment on the Regency Hotel, where the power breakfast originated. When the segment was finished, I told him that my idea of a power breakfast is breakfast in bed. That's real power—not having to get up for it!

Generally, my breakfast consists of seasonal fresh fruit, which my chef, Walter, has cut and arranged beautifully on my plate. It looks like a picture every morning. I have either a muffin or bread, courtesy of Beatrice, and cappuccino. I also make a mixed cold cereal, combining all the things that I think are healthy, or, in the winter, hot oatmeal with fruit puree.

Of course, a proper bed tray is essential; without it, eating in bed is not only no fun, it might get very messy. The one I have is a traditional classic breakfast tray. By the way, this is truly my bed pictured, and, yes, this is really the way I have breakfast every morning.

BLUEBERRY MUFFINS

YIELD: 1 DOZEN LARGE MUFFINS

I have made these for the last twenty-five years and I still have not found a way to improve them. The secret is not to overmix, so be sure to mix the batter by hand.

2 cups flour, sifted
1/2 teaspoon salt
1 tablespoon baking powder
1/2 cup sugar
1 egg
1/2 cup milk
1/2 cup light cream

Annemarie's breakfast tray: a tempting plate of fresh fruit, orange juice, and a pot of coffee, served with her favorite Sonia rose

4 tablespoons melted butter

1¼ cups fresh blueberries, washed, dried, and picked over to remove stems and leaves

Preheat oven to 400° F.

Into a mixing bowl, sift flour, salt, baking powder, and sugar. Set aside.

Beat egg until light and lemon-colored. Add milk, cream, and butter. Mix well.

Make a well in the center of the flour mixture. Pour in the egg and milk mixture all at once and mix just enough to moisten the dry ingredients. Fold in the berries.

Pour batter into a well-greased muffin pan, filling each cup about ⅔ full. Bake for about 25 minutes.

BREAKFAST CEREAL

SERVES: 1

THIS is my idea of a muësli. It has all the things I need to make me feel healthy, and when I go for *healthy*, I go all the way. This cereal should cover me for everything.

I always make fifteen servings of the recipe and keep them individually packed in the refrigerator.

¼ cup rolled oats
2 tablespoons wheat germ, toasted
½ tablespoon flaxseed
½ tablespoon millet
½ tablespoon sesame seeds
1 tablespoon sunflower seeds
1 tablespoon pumpkin seeds
1 tablespoon raisins
5 almonds, coarsely chopped
4 prunes, coarsely chopped
1 tablespoon chopped hazelnuts

Combine all ingredients. Serve cold with fresh fruit. Milk or plain yogurt may be added.

SMOOTHIE

SERVES: 1

THIS is a great quick breakfast that still gives you good nutrition.

1 cup orange juice
1 banana
5 strawberries
3 ice cubes

Pour orange juice into a blender. Add remaining ingredients and blend until smooth.

Acknowledgments

Just as a great recipe consists of many ingredients, so this book has been prepared with the talent, time, and care of many different people.

My deep appreciation goes to Bill Margerin, who, assisted by Richard Erhardt, took the beautiful photographs that made the food come alive; to Delores Custer, who styled the food so beautifully, helped by her assistants Vincent Beckley and Mariann Sauvion, who ran all over town to hunt down the perfect ingredients; and to Margaret Groves, who found just the right plates and accessories to highlight the food. Villeroy & Boch generously loaned us its beautiful china, and Josef van Kerckerinck, president of the Lucky Star Ranch Corp., came all the way from Chaumont, New York, to make sure we had a generous supply of his fabulous venison for our Christmas picture.

Thanks to the designers at Abrams: to Ray Hooper, who at the beginning of this project took infinite pains to set the book on the right path, and pulled all of us together in the process; to Dana Sloan, who oversaw the designing of the book; and to Rhea Braunstein, who made it look so beautiful. Thanks also to Naomi Warner, Darlene Geis, and Sam Antiput, who put such enthusiasm into getting the project started at Abrams.

Immeasurable thanks also go to the people who help me daily to create magic in my dining room: to Heidi Glocksien, who has been my right arm for thirteen years; to Maria Silva, who keeps the crystal sparkling and the linens crisp on every table; to Joe Nelson, who feels about the flowers he arranges as I do about my food—the love shines through in every arrangement; and to my chef, Walter Wakefield Poole, who has spoiled me forever with the breakfasts, lunches, and dinners he made for me: I will remember them always. To Kevin Gee, who helped me organize my dining room at the beginning and taught me all he knew about bar service; to Lizzie Bravo, who organized my office and business so that I could take the time to do this book. Special thanks go to Edna Smith, who has been with me for fifteen years, almost from the beginning.

And, of course, to my coauthor, Thelma Negley, who for close to two years arranged her time to accommodate my hectic schedule in order to work on this book. Last but not least, to Lory Frankel, my editor, who helped to make this a better book.

My special gratitude goes to Jacqueline Kennedy Onassis, who changed my life forever.

INDEX